Dedicated to my sister Terry

Preface
"Why I Write"

I write because God puts things in my heart, but I also write because like everyone else I go through things on a daily basis, things that need to be released. Some others can often relate, others not so much, but most of the time, I find my experiences are not unique. This is a good thing, a wonderful thing in fact, that I know I will never truly have to experience anything alone, as somewhere out there, a person who has or is going through the exact same conundrum exists.

But what do we do when that knowledge just doesn't suffice. Some of my loneliest experiences are being in a room full of people, even around ones that I truly love. There isn't much worse than the helpless, broken feeling of being the only miserable person in a happy room. I can't count the number of times I have been in the company of friends and get overwhelmed by a wave a depression that takes me to a world where no one else exists. It is just me and my sadness, for no particular reason. She likes to get me alone to feed me sinister lies about how useless and broken beyond repair I am. Sometimes I am strong and fight back valiantly, other times I succumb as she pushes the knife in deeper with every sweet, sadistic falsity she whispers in my ear.

I have a love hate relationship with my depression, on one hand it is my biggest challenge and has brought me way too close to the edge far too many times, and on the other hand it's strangely familiar and comfortable. It reminds me that I'm alive and tends to spark my creativity, unfortunately most of that is drowned out by frustration and painfully low self-worth. It's my least favorite part of who I am and also tends to be a defining factor. This is why I write, to relieve myself from this inner sickness that broods when I don't

.I always feel better every time I finish that last keystroke. Like maybe I did something for the better, or a weight has been lifted. Often the feeling is so intense I find I have to get up and do something else for a while and leave the editing for a later time. Yes, this is therapeutic for me, and maybe it can be for you too.

I write because there are things that need to be told, stories about the human experience to be accounted for. Right now I am only speaking from my life, but I really hope that changes soon, as I am just as interested in telling another's story. There are lessons to be learned in every person's experience and the desire to connect is naturally and biologically coded into our being.

We need to hear from others and share with others to get a sense of belonging, inspiration and encouragement.

I write because I have a hunger to consume words, the more I release the more I desire to take in, thus starting on a maddening cycle of filling and releasing that frankly, I truly love. There is something magical about getting lost in a story, living through the perspective of a completely different individual. It's the best way to escape and experience things we might not get to on our own.

I write because I have a need to express myself. Often there isn't someone around to listen, or maybe I get too nervous when I start speaking and forget where I originally planned to go. This way I get all the benefit of telling someone, with the added amount of freedom to rewrite and reread. Sometimes what seems like a good idea in my head ends up being junk on paper, so it is a good way to weed through the nonsense and get straight to the heart. We all have a need to release pent up emotion and display our creativity, the goal is to find an outlet that works for you.

I write because something inside me tells me to write, whether that is of myself or of God I don't know, but if I don't release these words I don't feel okay. Maybe it's a self-esteem thing or a purpose thing, either way I am glad it exists. There is something freeing about acting on things that come from our subconscious, the good things that is. I get plenty of urges I don't and should not act on, which is the beauty of having the ability to make decisions based on logic and reasoning, rather than pure instinct. It is pretty wild if you sit back and think about all the intricate parts that go into the human mind, be careful to not go too far down the rabbit hole though, I can be a frightening place.

I write because I have things to say. This is not me bragging, but I have experienced quite a few things in my life, not to mention things I have learned from spending time with other people. Not that my experience is more valuable than others, but it might be unique and interesting to some. Who knows, maybe I am just living in a bubble and this is the way I am supposed to find out that I am really not special. The words come naturally though, I don't force it. Every session I begin with a prayer for guidance and meditation on what inside of me needs to speak. If I don't get a response I take a break and come back later.

I write because I believe in the deepest part of my heart that this can help somebody. When I pray for direction on topics to write on I often get the feeling that this was particularly selected for one individual. I have learned to listen to this inclination in hopes that I am doing a service to my fellow man. Whether that person gets to it or not is out of my hands, my job is just to release.

I write because I want to encourage people to chase their dreams. This is a dream for me, something I kept buried deep within myself, and hopefully by doing this, by telling my story of where I came from and what I came through, that someone else may think, "hey If he can lay it all on the line then so can I."

That's why I loved teaching dance, you get so many kids coming in saying I want to be like x when I grow up. How cool is that, I literally get to help people chase their dreams!

I do this because I want to encourage. No matter what you have done, where you have been, and what you have been through, there is a purpose for your existence. I don't know what it is, and maybe you don't either, but if it is something to do with helping others, that is the best place to start. Start exploring yourself. If you could do anything what would it be? If you had enough money to support yourself and all of your family forever, what would you do? Start there, even if you aren't good at first. Passion, determination and willingness to work will take you so much further than raw talent any day. You can do it, I believe in you! Don't get discouraged when you don't get the results you want either. Trust me I get upset every time I open my account and see that literally no one has viewed my posts, but I continue and persevere anyways, because I know that this vision I have didn't come from myself. Finding a guiding force in your life, whatever that may look like, is probably the single most important factor to living a fulfilling life. We have to find that reason to wake up in the morning and work hard, a reason outside of supporting my tomorrow. At some point we will all leave this earth, what a shame it would be to leave not having answered the big question, what am I really here for?

Chapter

Wildflowers

Wildflowers under my skin, lightning
does not know how to strike and so it sinks
to where my hips meet the dip in my
waist -- here rivers tear themselves apart
into nameless pieces swallowing bodies
every day. A graveyard built on my bones,
but it's okay because anything covered
in ivy is pretty enough and I wish I was
covered in ivy too – bricks too red like
summertime shadows like winter lights
that don't understand the shapes they
carve into my skin, uncoil yourself from
me, stone is safer on my back than your
hands because this city has no heart
for me to burn holes into -- no hands to
dig my name into the ground, cold
unflinching weather does not say my
name the way you do and alleys know
my secrets but only so long as the wind
will stay – tell me the taste of the sounds
in the back of my throat and tell me my
hands are not soft enough, tell me my
words are too gory and too dangerous
and too much for your lungs to want
to hold, tell me my bones are too fragile,
or don't, and later I will pretend I never saw it coming.
And, still there are Wildflowers under my skin.

Pomegranate

A woman walks by the bench I'm sitting on
with her dog that looks part Lab, part Buick,
stops and asks if I would like to dance.
I smile, tell her of course I do. We decide
on a waltz that she begins to hum.

We spin and sway across the street in between
parked cars and I can tell she realizes
she chose a man who understands the rhythm
of sand, the boundaries of thought. We glide
and Fred and Ginger might come to mind or
a breeze filled with the scent of flowers of your choice.
Coffee stops flowing as a waitress stares out the window
of a diner while I lead my partner back across the street.

When we come to the end of our dance,
we smile at each other and to repay the favor
I tell her to be careful since the world comes to an end
three blocks to the east of where we stand. Then
I remind her as long as there is a '59 Cadillac parked
somewhere in a backyard between here and Boise
she will dance again.

As she leaves content with her dog, its tail wagging
like gossip, I am convinced now more than ever

that I once held hundreds of roses in my hands
the first time I cut open a pomegranate.

The Little Ghost

I knew her for a little ghost
    That in my garden walked;
The wall is high—higher than most—
    And the green gate was locked.

And yet I did not think of that
    Until she was gone—
I knew her by the broad white hat,
    All ruffled, she had on.

By the dear ruffles round her feet,
    By her small hands that hung
In their lace mitts, austere and sweet,
    Her gown's white folds among.

I watched to see if she would stay,
    What? She would like to—and oh!
She looked as if she liked the way
    I let my garden grow!

She bent above my favorite mint
    With conscious garden grace,
She smiled and smiled—there was no hint
    Of sadness in her face.

She held her gown on either side
    To let her slippers show,
And up the walk she went with pride,
    The way great ladies go.

And where the wall is built in new
    And is of ivy bare
She paused—then opened and passed through
    A gate that once was there

So Much Happiness

It is difficult to know what to do with so much happiness.
With sadness there is something to rub against,
a wound to tend with lotion and cloth.
When the world falls in around you, you have pieces to pick up,
something to hold in your hands, like ticket stubs or change.

But happiness floats.
It doesn't need you to hold it down.
It doesn't need anything.
Happiness lands on the roof of the next house, singing,
and disappears when it wants to.
You are happy either way.
Even that you once lived in a peaceful tree house
and now live over a quarry of noise and dust
cannot make you unhappy.
Everything has a life of its own,
it too could wake up filled with possibilities
of coffee cake and ripe peaches,
and love even the floor which needs to be swept,
the soiled linens and scratched records . .

Since there is no place large enough
to contain so much happiness,
you shrug, you raise your hands, and it flows out of you
into everything you touch. You are not responsible.
You take no credit, as the night sky takes no credit
for the moon, but continues to hold it, and share it,
and in that way, be known

Making Sure

To call your grandma,
your mother, your brother, your aunt
Listen closely
To the stories you've heard a thousand times,
their voice, their laugh,
Catalog how their thoughts shift from
one sentence to another, their little pauses in between,
And never hang up too soon.
For the cruelest thing in this world is
the surprise of the swift knock
of death on a door
How quickly the loved ones that once dotted your life
and your telephone line can become
Guilt ridden memories
of the phone calls
you wish you would have made.

Silence

around me a silence so serene
so completely innocent
that I feel wrapped inside
forever
I see a dog barking at me
cars passing me by
girls laughing
but all remains unheard though noticed
I live in a visual world
a soundless theater
a totally different approach of
communication
written and watched
but nonetheless showing me
the bright and the dark side
of humanity

Vespertine

The lady she was
Of pale and darkness
She grew to be of nature's kindness
        Threw shadows she roamed
        And weaved into smut
    Though vigorous a lady she dashed to progress
Her mind sought hatred
Her heart the same
But everyone knew her soul was of kindness
        Her color of blacks
        And her visions of grey
        The title she holds Dominatrix of Darkness
She vigorously smears
And seldom she cheers
For that is her balky boldness
        Frightening she was
        Trade of all trades
        Transforming children,
            mother to motherless

Gone too Soon
(To Tom)

This has been bringing up
a lot of things about my past.
I remember how I would tell myself,
that my only wish was to lie still,
underground and lifeless.
Now I can only heavily
regret my words.
I remember when Grandma died,
and didn't even get a chance to say goodbye,
nor to get to know her.
I do remember all of the moments
I thought of death as my only way
out of this shithole of a place.
 Now we are all mourning for a loss
that happened way too soon.
He was goodness in creature,
a reminder of good nature as human beings.
He deserved so much better.
May you rest in peaceful eternity.

Continuum

(To Carlos)

Filaments of his gift
Persistent mysteries
Beauteous bouquet of flowers
Palpable consciousness
A world of naming
Of ablutions in time
Fighter instinct action
Persistent and precise order
The pressing in
Closing in the heart thrums for a powerful image
Dazzling light: redemption!
To reassess language, it's tactility
Emotion,
(emotionless)
lyric,
(lyrical)
oblique irony twists,
(of his mind body and soul)
Shifts by pulse and ear,
Resilient! His consummate body poetics
echo into the night
It hits us: what is now absent
from every bouquet are
cut like flowers before their time

The Past

"Sometimes,
I shrink into my past so deeply
it is hard for me to come up
to the surface again.

the past holds tight onto me
(or perhaps I'm holding tight onto my past)
and honestly,

sometimes I let it get to me.
see, nostalgia is a good hell of a liar.
nothing was as good as it wants me to believe it was
and certainly,
there is nothing I can do to go back in time.
so, I might as well miss you as long as eternity lasts;
at least I'll be able to write about you until forever."

Spiritual Infants

this darkness knows no borders
we're free as birds,
if only our minds weren't cages we would follow the
path of heartless soldiers, see the earth
wrapped in scorching faces

why are the mornings so heavy?
the sun beams with indifference
watching us die as…

"spiritual infants"

At 4:00 pm. On March 12th, I wrote this.

I am reliving past lives,
In order to distract from mine,
Endlessly running out of time,
From playing catch up in my mind,
Unsaying words I should never have said,
Force them down my throat, I catch my breath,
Still they play in surround sound in my head,
A monotone I've grown to dread,
Every undone knot, tangles again,
Each new day, feels like the end,
And lately it's getting harder to pretend,
It'll all work out 'ok'

Hide

I know you're nothing like them, you're too thoughtful, too sensible to be like them, I don't want you to be ashamed of yourself, being sensitive is not a curse,

you have a heart, and this heart is too soft and delicate, and so you feel, you feel and that's nothing to be ashamed of.

Stop hiding your true self, it's way more beautiful than theirs, I want you to stop talking like them, and start talking like you, to stop dressing like them and start dressing like you,

I want you to stop wanting to be like them and start being you. And I'm not trying to be cliché and tell you you're perfect just the way you are or anything like that, I'm just saying that I know you have an unimaginably beautiful heart.

I don't want you to hide that, just because everybody else isn't like you. You don't have to be like them, by any means, especially when you're so special like that.

I am nothing

I am nothing. I'm sitting here in a hospital bed with not a single flower or balloon or cheap stuffed bear in sight. The only people to come into my room have been a doctor, a nurse, and a group of medical students. The group of students shuffled in quietly when, as far as they know, I was asleep. When one young man asked about the cause of his diagnosis..." yes he said,

look...at... the... *wounds*", the surgeon with them whispered "suicide" like he was a little boy scared someone would hear him swear. One girl lingered until I opened my eyes and said "Boo!" to get some privacy. I couldn't help but noticing just a bit too many bruises and cuts on her arms. Maybe if I still felt remorse I would've regretted scaring her, she looked almost sad when I did. Oh well, that's not my problem.

When I walked out of the hospital doors today there were plenty of people waiting but none for me. As I walked down the crowded streets of Chicago to go home I got called a boy twice but only a girl once. I celebrated alone at a bar after changing into a binder a button up, and some jeans. Oh how I missed the pinching in my ribs of a binder. It'll have to do though, I can barely afford my studio, much less top surgery. At the bar a man and woman got into a fight whether I was male or female. I instructed them to calm their titties and man-titties because 1. It isn't any of their business 2. Neither of them will find out and 3. My gender doesn't matter to them. They walked away squabbling about it like children; anyways not giving a damn about what I said.

    Do you see now? I am nothing. These two days both prove that fact. No one cares about me and I don't care about them.

    I am happy....I am nothing.

ABC's of Love

A)ccepts you as you are.

(B)elieves in you.

(C)alls you sometimes just to cheer you up and say: 'Hello!'

(D)oesn't give up on you.

(E)nvisions the whole of you, even the hidden and unfinished parts.

(F)orgives your mistakes.

(G)ives unconditionally.

(H)elps you.

(I)nvites you into their life and space.

(J)ust accompanies you on your pathway through life.

(K)eeps you close at heart.

(L)oves you for who you are and not what you have.

(M)akes a difference in your life(N)ever Judges.

(O)ffers support

(P)icks you up when you're down.

(Q)uiets your fears.

(R)aises your spirits.

(S)ays only good things about you, but also

(T)ells you the truth whenever this is necessary.

(U)nderstands you.

(V)alues you.

(W)alks beside you.

(X)-plains things you don't understand.

(Y)ells when you won't listen and

(Z)aps you into the higher realities of our earthly existence.

Midnight and shoelaces

i don't want to mention death
any more than we do the weather

                                        whatever daily obituaries
                                            and fahrenheit levels
                                                 consume us both

                our shoelaces are untied
          while walking and people are watching

                    no matter the weather
                      no matter the month

when   the   temperature   drops   we   go
coffin shopping at the pink and gold house

                    we cruise control the drive home
                    so to stare at the faces of the lonely

midnight is the eye of expressions
    of the people who do not love us now
        didn't love us then

                and never will

because   we   don't   know   any   better
we   talk   it   up;   a   series   of   consequences
up to the effects of obligations

        midnight and shoelaces are the only theories
           the lazy idioms understood

      we are grounded by strenuous greetings
        about astrology and the occult

                when i joke about being garbage

it is because i am a joke about being garbage
and garbage is   as
garbage does

          isn't it amazing

             to make you
          to make you want me
        to make you want to touch me

wanting is the melting of the ego
wanting is the witnessing of melting
melting can be spontaneous and romantic
at midnight when your shoelaces are finally tied

just so you know:
when i want something – I ask for it

        "your shoelaces are untied and it's midnight So
            I must leave"

Your Peeling Skin

Whenever
we talk,
I never seem to get
my message across
but I always hear
your transmission
loud & clear playing non-
stop.

I want to smell
your peeling skin
in the hottest Texas Summer.

I want to drink
your tears
like I wandered the desert
forty years.

I want you
to wake up in darkness
so long you wonder
if you'll ever peel again.

You laugh as I
pour gasoline
onto these pages and taunt
you with struck matches I let burn
to my fingertips.

Burn

You smirk and say,
"Nothing can hurt me
anyways. I don't even
hear you
anymore."

I started to speak,
but after what you said…

I'll burn these pages
instead.

Toxic

If you're thinking of going back to a toxic relationship, or keep going back and leaving continuously, this is your reminder *not* to do that, especially if it's affecting your other relationships and friendships. Don't fight for someone that hurts you and disregard those that want the best for you. It isn't romantic. It's not true. It's not cute. It's not passionate. It's sad and unhealthy and awful and tiring, and you're stronger than that. The cycle won't end. They won't change. And, even though you miss them, however terribly, you have to walk away. You go back and you're making it seem like it's no big deal. You go back and your word starts to mean nothing. You go back and you're part of the problem. You aren't "fighting for them" or "giving everything you've got." Instead you're draining yourself for someone that doesn't care. You're distancing yourself from real love for someone that doesn't adore you like you should be adored. You deserve better than that. Stop succumbing to the loneliness and renewing the pain, because it will go away if you leave it alone long enough.

Trinity Guidance

If I screech and cry deep inside
Will it suffocate the fears living within me
Fears that are profound and buried into my soul
In this peaceful silent night I grow weary
Amputated limbs and mutilated hearts
Red scrawls of blood
And eight legged freaks
Dynamic running,
crawling slowly
into infinity
thundering shrieks
I'm losing my mind
the apparent parent
it's spiritual guidance
my spiritual trinity
Oh! Help me Lord
I'm on my knees

"in the name of The Father, The Son and the Holy Spirit"

Oh! Please

Amen

Beyond a doubt

Amen

Without certainty

Amen

Hear my prayer

Trinitarian guidance of thee, for me

No heartbeat I feel and no eyes to see

My thoughts are haunting to a simmering Hell

I can't hear a thing except that screeching bell

Try to release but no movement appears

The Holy trinity has brought me to tears

Amen Amen

Clouds, white and fluffy

Amen Amen

Angels are dancing

Amen Amen

I see the Kingdom

Amen Amen

Of my Trinity guidance

... Hazel Eyes

You leaned your forehead against mine and grazed the tip of my nose with yours as your lips moved toward mine. Before you kissed me, those hazel eyes locked with mine and lingered there, as if to convey what your words could not. The harsh edges of your narrow eyes softened. You looked at me like I was the most valuable treasure in the world, a look made me feel you were afraid of losing me. This didn't happen often, but it always surprised me, a little like you. All I could do was kiss you back, inhaling slowly as I pressed my lips against yours. I still can't explain the warmth that touched my heart when your eyes caught mine or the fluttering in my stomach when our lips finally met.

Love is...

Love is a large part of my life.

And, I mean… I write about everything else. Why not love? Of course love.

Love should be neither inconspicuous nor apologetic.

Love shouldn't hide nor should it apologize for itself.

Love is life, nothing more and nothing less.

Scars

I used to cut
my skin yes
what matters is I used to cut my soul
I used to tear down my spirit
flesh by flesh
fiber by fiber

I saw my soul and de-humanized it
it was of no importance
it did not matter
and I almost killed it
on the outside it seemed fine
happy
content
beautiful even
but that was not the case
it was a liar
because it really was not alright
it was dying
and as the blood dripped from my side
my soul slowly dripped with it
like a steady waterfall of pain
but this is no sad story
my soul did not die
I learned to like it
my soul my scars

Post-Diagnosis

reason:

                                              unreason:

the brain is

                                              an unlit synagogue

easily charted

                                              in dark waters

using machines

                                              it can baffle faith

& therapy

                                              can asphyxiate

don't worry

                                              the drowning dogs

 your pretty head

                                              painted for the gods

it's simple

                                              to rage & riot & rot

to manage

                                              the vacant parking lot

with the appropriate

                                              knives   do what some

medicines

                                              can not

Me (to be)

Isn't it funny?

When I meet

Someone new
One of the
first questions
I ask is "what
Do you want
To be when
You "grow up"?
And they look
At me in a

Funny way

And tell me:

"I'm a teacher"

Sp3ctrum

I am the modern-day Morpheus
And I am here to proclaim my innocence
I made the minutes disappear
Within
hours and minutes from seeing the spectrum
I am thin, an errant swarm of bees
a naked lunatic
faithful
selfish
old
 a tiger with adumbration to man and sufferings likes bridges
collapsing on bridges
immensely strong

a tiger with adumbration to man
and sufferings likes bridges collapsing on bridges
immensely strong

a wild beast
a paradox of authenticity
me
racy
rage
murder
red
spectrum of the nebulous
spectrum of the now
spectrum of a current lion being mauled by Morpheus
the blood is crimson
glistens and luminous
and drips
until
the spectrum fades away

the spectrum goes slowly
with brilliance of aire
for
I, the tiger the lion and the bees
I (Morpheus), the spectrum has just begun.

Children of the 'Sp3ctrum'

children of the machines
we have learned to forget
because we didn't want to remember
.

mind cloaked in amnesia
and maybe we realized
what we can't remember
can't hurt us
and we chased anomalous patterns
of thought
into the darkest shade of
the night wondering why
things have to be this way
with the past reduced to
nothing but whispers of
shattered images sucked
into the bottomless void

Black and White

Black and white
I think about all the memories day and night
My days are black and white
But the memories of those good old days burn bright
Black and white
At the end of the tunnel I see a light
When things do not go right that light shines bright
When the path is not right then turn left, but if there's nothing left, then trust the light which is in your sight.
Black and white
I may seem black and white
But there are some parts to my life which I keep out of sight

They say "out of sight, out of mind",
but what if my mind is out
of my own sight?
Control your mind before it controls your life, but let go of control and find the hidden joys that life hides. Put on your shining armor and become your own dark knight. Turn your darkness into shining glamour
Your glamour and honor is
hidden in your sense of humor

You were always more

reaching past the finite

into abstract blues blending

aquas into cobalt

your sea washes into my sky

filtering our light

into a merge beyond everyday

love that soars

into the vastness of our own

infinity

inked on a musical palette

of breaths between waves

where I drift with you

Bleeding Hearts

Isn't the heart's
sole job to bleed?
I tried searching within our conversation
For the word "love"
And from our September 16th
Correspondence
There are thirty-four mentions
Of it alone
Thirty-three from the 15th
Twenty-three from the 15th
nine from the 12th
I just wish that I'd known
That nothing is exponential

Rose

Was it me?

Did I scare you away with my thorns?

Or were my petals too vibrant of a red?

Did my unfurling petals come off too bold?

Or was my perfume too much of a stench?

Listen to me, young man.

You don't find a rose like me everyday on the street.

Either pick me or leave me be. And that's a final request.

my silly equivocal thoughts I endure between midnight and one in the morning

Maybe   I'm awake at midnight or-
Maybe   this is just a dream.
Maybe   this is what turning a corner feels like -
        and sinking into wet cement.
Maybe   this is my fault.
Maybe   the curse followed us home from our New Orleans trip.
Maybe   the medicine woman is right -
        skinning a yearling rabbit would help,
        or burning sage in each corner of the house.
Maybe   that's the sound of my resolve breaking.
Maybe   it's the condom.
Maybe   my therapist, Dr. Peterson who looks like Charleze Theron on crack is smart -
        I haven't spent enough 'me time' yet.
Maybe   therapy won't be necessary.
Maybe   you lied to me. Worse,
Maybe   you didn't.
Maybe   it was an accidental overdose.
Maybe   it's only possible to love a memory.
Maybe   you're right – everything comes to a bitter end.
Maybe   Boy George is really a genius -
        because…I'll tumble 4 U
Maybe   there's no room for us.
Maybe   instead of a gun you choose…strong chord
        Maybe   my babysitter was right-
        all you have to do is go in, shut the door,
        go poopy and wipe

Maybe I forgot to wash my hands.
Maybe every time I start to type that "f*** off" text

I think of how you clipped my toenails and put them in two perfectly neat piles.

Maybe I double my dosage tonight.
Maybe it's not as accidental as I tell you.
Maybe I move to Las Vegas, get a job as a street performer.
Maybe I stop running for once and hold my ground.
Maybe that's why I always lose at chess: impatience.
Maybe I take the batteries out of the smoke alarm and always forget where I put the new ones .
Maybe only then does the fire start.
Maybe I want your body, soaking wet and wrapped around mine like a bandage.
Maybe when I kiss the next person, I swallow their soul.
Maybe I shave my head, smear it with ash, Catholicism is just an exercise
Maybe Dr. Peterson is right again. That's why I am alone
Maybe I'll be alone forever eating skittles and mac-n-cheese and playing Yahtzee with myself and singing old Culture Club songs

A Featherless Bird

Splintered, scattered, scraped. I want to fly away; but I am just a featherless bird.

- Hello?

I slowly articulate my words into the phone pressed against my ear.

- I know no one cares, but I'm going to kill myself. I just can't take it anymore. The voices in my head are yelling at me. I want them to stop. I want it all to stop. Please help me.

- I'm here to help. But first, what is your name?

I ignore the operator's interrogation and continue to talk as the cold wind howls through my short-cropped hair.

- I feel as though my lifeless body is just hanging in the balance, readily waiting for god's hand to push me over the edge.

- Please breathe and take a step back, try to compose yourself. You're no longer alone, I am listening to you. I understand what you are going through.

- You don't understand, no one does. How could they? I am just another meaningless grain of solar dust, floating through space and time. You say you are listening but you don't seem to hear me. I just want to fly and jump into the abyss. Free from all of this world's meaningless restraints. I am sick; too sick to be helped. I don't even know why I bothered to call. As if someone on the other end of this phone could care more for me in this glimmer of a moment than every person who has dared to cross paths with me.

I take a deep breath before I continue speaking. I ask the operator for her name. I guessed that it was a her by her pitch. She tells me that her name is Cynthia.

- I know a Cynthia.

- Really?

- Yeah, she was some family friend or something, I can't really remember exactly who though.

Before I can further explore this newfound knowledge, Cynthia interrupts me.

- It sounds windy where you are. Are you safe?

I glance down at the street 53 stories below me. It's littered with people who are busy doing their regular chores on this brisk Saturday afternoon. A cab. A lot of cabs actually. There is so much yellow it's almost as though the sun has moved to the ground. From atop the bright yellow taxis gleam the sun's rays; hundreds hitting me all at once. After snapping out of my brief illusion, I answer Cynthia's question.

- Let's just say that, if I fall now, they'll be scrapping my remains off the sidewalk with a shovel

I kick my right shoe off. 1...2...3...4...5...almost 6 seconds before my shoe thuds against the hard ground below me. This is it for me.

- I know what you guys say. But it's all just a bunch of words to you.

- What do you mean by that?

- I mean, are you telling me not to jump off this goddamn building because you want me to survive, or because another dead statistic looks bad on your company records?

- I want you to survive, I really do. Losing you will weigh on my mind for the rest of my life. I have lost people before and I don't want to add your name to the list.

- So I'm just another name on a list huh? Is that really all I am to you? Some sort of souvenir that you can scratch onto your "should've, could've, would've" note?

- That's not it, I do-

- Lies! I don't believe a word of it. As a matter of fact, I called because I wanted you to know that you've failed twice now.

- How is that?

- My brother jumped off this same building two years ago today and you couldn't do anything to help him.

There was a long pause before I continued.

- I couldn't do anything to help him...

The operator remains quiet for a bit and we both sit in silence, seemingly waiting for some other person to join in on our conversation and fill the growing void of silence between us. - Finally, the operator addresses me in a calm voice, with no sense of urgency or panic.

- Are you on top of the Johnson Enterprise Tower?

- How did-

- My cousin jumped off that building two years ago to this day.

My heart fell and I wondered who exactly I was talking to. I couldn't be. It can't be. I never met my father and only my brother met his fam-, Cynthia cuts through my thoughts like a hot knife through butter.

- I know this might sound crazy, but was your brother named James McArthur?

This tangent only lasted for so long. Who cares if she was some lost relative. In that moment she was nothing but another liar and hypocrite. Her words of love and care mean nothing to me.

- Please stay on the line. Don't hang up.

- I won't hang up, but you're going to sound silly talking to some broken piece of plastic on the other end.

- What do you mean by that?

I stand up. 6 seconds. That's all it takes. I take a step into the looseness of the air in front of me. The gravity around me sucks me towards the ground. Wind rushes. Hard. People yell and point as my soon to be lifeless corpse falls from the sky above their heads. A phone line goes silent and an operator cries at her desk.

 Splintered, scattered, scraped. Finally I fly away, a featherless bird.

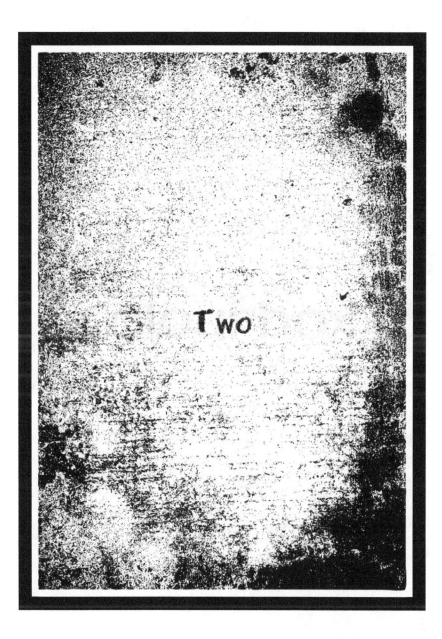

Breaking the Mold

"Break the mold of the image hidden deep in the subconscious that sharply cuts reality in pretty boxes of You vs The Others. Cut the picture of survival of the fittest in half and notice how when you put the torn pieces back together they don't align to match. Society lies to soft, pretty boys, demands them to be tough. Society lies to sturdy, wide-shouldered girls, offends them till they're numb, with pictures of petite, long-haired models who smile widely at the passersby, as if all those people are is beauty. Breathe beauty, exude beauty, wake up and sleep with beauty. So we give our souls to Satan or the salesman to provide us with beauty in small, affordable doses. Droplets of potential, just enough to guarantee you coming back the next day for more. Break the mold. Crumble the perfectly round cookies you made into dust and assemble them again with weird angles sticking out sharp. Sharp, sharply poking at their space of existence. Ugly when considering today's standards. Crumble them up, reshape them and tell me; do they not still taste the same?"

Waste of Space

I don't even know what I'm doing anymore. I no longer care about my health, or my happiness, or anything else. I don't even know why I'm still alive, here, breathing right now. I have no motivation to do anything anymore. The daily stress is killing me inside, and all the questions, all of the doubts, everything, it just makes me slowly slip onto my old habits again.

Do you ever feel like you're losing your mind?? Losing track of time and losing every single thing you've ever had? Like every single string inside of you broke. And it feels like being cracked open, hurts like hell, but you in the end of the day feel numb.

I'm faithless and tired of living through people's expectations. I can't be what they want me to be. I can't follow the system they want me to follow. mistake. It breaks you, and it takes your sanity away, and it makes you feel smothered and out of your mind, running out of control. Everything I once thought I would be is falling apart. I can't take it anymore And it feels like everything I do it's just another.

I'm in a mess. And I don't believe I'll ever be okay again. Sorrow is the only thing I've got left. I'll live every day of my life just because I have to not, because I want to...

I am a waste of space.

LiveLoveLife

The Years have passed by,
In the blink of an eye,
Moments of sadness,
And joy have flown by.

People I loved,
Have come and have gone,
But the world never stopped,
And we all carried on.

Life wasn't easy,
And the struggles were there,
Filled with times that it mattered,
Times I just didn't care.

I stood on my own,
And I still found my way,
Through some nights filled with tears,
And the dawn of new days.

And now with old age,
It's become very clear,
Things I once found important,
Were not why I was here.

And how many things,
That I managed to buy,
Were never what made me,
Feel better inside.

And the worries and fears,
That plagued me each day,
In the end of it all,
Would just fade away.

But how much I reached out,
To others when needed,
Would be the true measure,
Of how I succeeded.

And how much I shared,
Of my soul and my heart,
Would ultimately be,
What set me apart.

And what's really important,
Is my opinion of me,
And whether or not,
I'm the best I can be.

And how much more kindness,
And love I can show,
Before the Lord tells me,
It's my time to go.

What If

what if I died yesterday
would anyone miss me today
what if I died yesterday
and never said goodbye
would you hate me because
I just wanted the pain to stop
what if I died yesterday
would you forget who I was
would you forget who I became
would you want to forget me today
what if I died yesterday
would you say good riddance
if you saw me lying there
no heartbeat or pulse
just a cold empty stare
what if I died yesterday
would you cry like I did
every single night
because today is today
and the memories wouldn't quit
what if I died yesterday
would you see my scars
and wish you would notice
how much pain I endured today
what if I died tomorrow

The Wind (part one)

The wind whispers and brings with it the scent of summer afternoons. Teasing kisses in balmy weather, the air from a ceiling fan doing nothing to cool off sweat from summer sex and dew. The wind brings with it the sweet scent of chocolate, of melted square pressed tongue to tongue, succulent sensations making us shiver on the sandy shore, an afternoon sweet treat to cap off our indulgent delight

The Circle of Grief

you arrive at my door
you arrive at my door in your birthday suit
you arrive at my door in that suit holding flowers
in your right hand
pink orange carnations
that you thrust in my face like a pompom
like a one-armed cheerleader, cheering me on

in your sleeves whole gardens
of chicanery [you arrive at my door]
what kind of man [naked]
are you/could you/can you
be? [holding flowers] for me? *are* they?

[you arrive] all I can see
are these flowers in my face
full of carnations gardenias in various ghosts of white
you are a particular ghost at my doorstep and somewhere in front
of me your voice
is an interruption, your face is nowhere your face/your voice/your
face/your voice

you arrive at my door holding a gardenia dead crow:
it's hurt you say
no, it's dead I say
can you fix it? you say
no, it's dead I say
do you want it? you say

here, give it here I say

I thank him and shut the door
The man
The man (in his birthday suit)
The man in the suit (at the door) grieving at his departure
Sadness prevails

The Wind (part two)

The wind howls and takes with it the scent of what I have left of you. I taste the breeze but all that's left is the bitterness of cacao, making me shiver against the cold embrace of air, a reminder that you're no longer there save for the chill and the aftertaste of what once was, the howling of the wind taunting me of what can never be.

Flowers, Moonlight & Breeze

crown me with flowers
dress me with moonlight
lavish me with the breeze

(& know in my "midnight", daggers will not hold should you do me wrong)

Kindness

Kindness is a present anyone can give.

Often it's as simple as a smile,

A nod and a word of understanding,

Taking time to chat for a while

Or sending a letter, a text or an e-mail.

    Such gifts anyone can bring

    Who thinks of us with a loving heart.

    Wrapped in the warmth that flows

    From the sender's inner world,

    Sets the days they're received apart.

What can I say

What can I say to cheer you up? This afternoon the sky is like five portholes between the clouds. The unidentifiable weeds are tall and still unidentifiable and I miss the cows in the field, where have they gone? Sometimes one would wander then stand in the middle of the road and I'd have to stop my car and wait for it to decide to finish crossing. I am drinking seltzer through a straw because of my injury and I have inexplicable bruises on the side of my thigh and I just spent the last five minutes watching a bird through my window sitting in the small crotch where two phone lines x together though it flew off before I could take a picture of it.

In the urgent care waiting room this morning there was a magazine with a proven neuroscience article on rituals that will make us happy and the first was practicing gratitude but when I tried to think of something right there next to the guy with the walker and the woman with gauze held to her cheek I came up blank. Because I am a terrible person I will tell you that my neighbor does this thing I hate with her kids called heart-bread, where they're forced each night before bed to go around one by one and come up with a moment of gratitude and I want to tell her that we can thank anything—the crushed cans in recycling, my wristwatch for keeping time, the rainstorm yesterday that had water pouring from the gutters.

I mean, we all overflow; we all feel an abundance of something but sometimes it's just emptiness: vacant page, busy signal, radio static, implacable repeat rut where the tone arm reaches across a spinning vinyl record to play it again, rest its delicate needle in a groove and caress forever the same sound from the same body. Which is to say that the opposite of ennui is excitement and I'm not feeling it either today, not even a little.

Not in the Walgreen's while browsing the shiny electric rainbow nail-polish display indefinitely while waiting for my prescription. And probably not on my run later no matter how bucolic the mountains seem in the 5pm heat. The second ritual in that article was to touch people, which is easy if you're with people you can touch but I'm in too loud a solitude and can only touch myself which reminds me of that old Divinyls' song and I'm pretty sure that's not what the article meant.

I think that I am actually writing about God. I think since this is not true of us because we all have bodies which make us small countries or maybe islands. If summer means our bodies are more porous perhaps we're also more open to this inexplicable sadness that hangs here from the cinderblocks, drags itself across the barbed wire fence. What I'm trying to tell you is that I'm not cheered up either. That bird, before it flew off, I like to think of the crossed wires, the impenetrable conversations rushing under it's feet.

你好嗎？

Say Nothing

Sometimes the most powerful words we can say is to say nothing. At times silence can be more potent than sound, and sometimes the best advice you can give is none at all. In my life I have found one of the most valuable tools we have in love is just to listen to another. Being present for someone can mean more than any gift or piece of advice we may have to offer.

Sometimes we just need to vent, we don't need advice or opinions, we just need another soul to hear us out. Seeing the healing from a person dumping out loads of pressure in front of my very eyes is incredibly magical. Witnessing a transformation before our very eyes is indescribable event and one of the coolest things we can experience. These are the rare moments I will never forget and times where clarity of purpose washes over me. Being the trusted handler of this confidential information may up meaning almost as much to you as to the speaker.

Take the time to check in with someone today, and don't take, "Yeah I'm doing okay," for an answer. Poke and prod, but don't be forceful, you never know that person may be ready to explode and you may be the lifeline they so desperately needed. Never be too focused that you are not ready to answer the call when God sends someone your way, you may miss out on an experience that will change your life. The bonding experience that can happen when you share your heart with another is incomparable. There is nothing more healing than one human pouring out their heart to another. Establish a deep, meaningful bond with someone because surely the day will come when you need someone to hear you out and you will have someone to turn to.

Never undermine the value you can add to another human by simply being there for them. Sometimes one does need much more than that, just a caring soul to hear them out. This takes no skill or experience, just an open heart and a quiet mind. Try it for yourself and see how rewarding it can be, who knows you might nhmake a new best friend.

Never undermine the value you can add to another human by simply being there for them. Sometimes one does need much more than that, just a caring soul to hear them out. This takes no skill or experience, just an open heart and a quiet mind. Try it for yourself and see how rewarding it can be, who knows you might make a new best

I saw and said nothing

The scars lined her wrist,
Both faded and new.
A small smile crossed her face
As though holding a secret only she knew.
Every movement graceful,
Every piece of her lovely self.
I wanted to speak up but,
She didn't even know me.

I wanted to ask for her story,
Wanted to ask her why.
Wanted to show her how similar they were,
How close her scars were to mine.
Yet I saw and said nothing
Staying seated in my chair.
Pretending not to know
Pretending they weren't there.

For to acknowledge her pain,
I must admit to mine, and
I could not bear to show my hurt or
To reveal I'm anything but fine.
I opened my mouth to speak,
To tell her I felt the same.
Yet just as swiftly it fell shut,
The words stuck inside my brain.

I tugged my sleeves further over my hands,
Desperately hiding my wrists.
The words bottled up inside me
Even as my hands curled into fists.
Sadness danced within her eyes,
Swirling in every forced smile.
A word of mine could spark hope in her gaze

Yet still, there I stayed, silent all the while.

It hurt to watch her feel alone,
To watch her demons roil and twist.
It ached to know I could ease her loneliness
Simply by baring my wrist.
Now I compose and I write this
Trying to assuage my guilt.
As though these words could compensate
For the things I never tried to say,
And the girl I never helped.

Perhaps it is arrogant,
To say I knew what pain burned inside.
Perhaps it would only have made it worse,
Telling her of the bloody tears I've cried.
Yet the part that seems the worst to me
Is knowing I never tried.

I hate what my demons have done to me,
Giving rise to self-hatred and life to untold pain.
See, I hate them not for breaking me, but rather
For spurring a fear so great, I cannot help those who hurt the same.

Lost in my mind,

Struggling to find the words to describe how I feel, the weight of my world crushes my chest, Making it harder and harder to breathe each time. Realities misgivings intensify, I wonder when this will stop, will I make it through? As the days, weeks, months go by, Hopelessness becomes all too familiar, I wonder why life brought me here, Struggling to hold on, I remain hanging, By a thread that should of snapped long ago, I am thankful for the support, however small, It keeps me from crashing to the ground. I pause for a long moment and reflect, taking in the stillness around me, I realize the commotion is within, Focusing on what is around me, Calmness starts to creep about, I embrace the calm and exhale a deep breath. Expelling all that was causing chaos within

Two Moons

Shape shift
with the stars
hiding in the universe
you make the sky
swirl,
your eyes
two moons
that call me,
make me leave
behind
my earthly home,
uprooted
and utterly
at your mercy
I stay
fixated
looking up
at the velvet sky,
the vastness
that is you,
and I'm just
a speck,
only a speck.

Trapped in Today

Trapped in today
Chasing tomorrow,
Searching…
For new beginnings.
I sit in golden silence
Listening…
For the whispers, of stars.

I eat overcooked lies,
Trying to cope with
Burning truths.
And still…
My darkest regrets
Stain my clean slate.

Redemption recedes.
Love returns, like a cancer.
Only to finish the job.
Last hopes dwindle…
Like a drowning flame.
Fear is The Darkness
salivating…
For my failure.

Waiting for me
To be at my weakest…
Waiting to feed.
But…
when we are left defenseless

We are meant to be our strongest.

The Lady Vespertine

She's there all the time with her poison apple soul
She can't help the fact that she's aging while you're young
white skin showing the blue map of her veins
and lips like five pink petals that she stole
unlike witches she could stop
peddling deadly combs
to scour the scalps with arsenic
and keep from turning old
She was there when I was young and pure
and there when I was hallucinating images
and spewing to me I wasn't beautiful
but a significant unique kind of person
it's beyond a doubt that she comes from a tribe
and she's transparent to all those vicious lies
Inside this trance she's held me for years
even when my hair burned like sulfur and grime
my skin crawled through and my eyes turned green
from time to time she would expel me from thee
there will always be the indestructible figure
but only she can tell a lie
before the truth of consequences
come marching in like rolling thunder
through the sullen skies of purity
the evil queen of this smuttin layered fairy tail
is none other than the late great Lady Vespertine
kindred guardian of Morpheus and this solid SP3CTUM
for which we are all sloths and gluten to she
the songstress of the curry savored soul

and the soft heated mind

"oh thee of colors with accents of shade"

she sang to the mistress of the lateral shadows
I believed her and when I asked if I could cut my hair she let me
When my skin broke out in red bumps she pretended not to see
Her portraits covered every wall and still she wept and wept
when the Mister went off to paint the village maids

Beauty doesn't make you indestructible
as once she thought her fierceness came to be.

Heart

there will always be mothers pleading with mirrors
this is my advice:
take your heart from your chest and examine it
let it bleed in your hands
talk to it softly as you might once have spoken to

a lover

or a white stag

or a mirror

do not take a bite
or try to choke her with it
sing to it
then return it
gently
to the empty
cavity of your chest

Myself Burning

sometimes i give in
to your voice which
still echoes in my ears
you've given me
a lifetime of whispers
filling up my mind
binding me
a rope
pulling me back
to the past
it's not over
won't be until
you leave my heart
can't you see i'm
trying to move on
let go
of my hand
because yours is
on fire
pour water
all over me
wake me up

i've woken up
my eyes are open

i can see
there's more to me than
your presence
i can light my own fires
without
burning myself
i promise
i won't forget

i couldn't if i tried but
give me a chance
to be alive
to live
now that i know i
deserve it
i won't settle
for less
so let me
go…please, let me go

Written in the Stars

Somewhere,

Somehow,

We'll find each other again,

Like the Moon gravitates to the Earth,

Slowly

Drawing closer,

Inch by inch

Until we destroy each other,

We won't have time to flinch,

Just a firey explosion

After the long waited anticipation,

There's no time

For any hesitation,

Countless millennials

Will we wait,

For the date

We collide,

Don't be afraid,

We'll be fine,

I promise you

We'll be written

In the stars too

(A child's) Reality

As a child, I thought promises were meant to be fulfilled
and "forever's" would last forever.
I thought everyone meant the words that came out from their mouths
and that people were actually happy if they had a smile on their face.
But I was wrong.

"I grew up and reality gave me a hard slap across my face to wake me up from a dream of a fool, to tell me that it was all wrong. All I saw was people yelling at each other with broken dreams and promises in their hands. They showed me that some forevers would last for not more than 3 seconds long. Then I saw how people spat out lies to mask up their true intentions and how most of them shone brightly with the prettiest smile on their face only to break down, to drown in their pain when no one was looking."

As a child,
 I was hopeful and happy.
But now, I am only trying my best just like everyone else.

Jungle Gym or Jim in the Jungle

I am James, Jimmy or Jim .
My dad is Timothy, Timmy or Tim
My mom is Kimberly, Kimmy, Kim.

I walk, walk, walk
With my teacher
And my class.
It's time for recess
So we're going to the gym.

This is my favorite part of school.
I wonder if today will be extra cool?

Wait -- I hear something!
What could that be?
What's that about?
What am I about to see?
One way to find out....

The sights I see are *so so* silly --
A gibbon wearing a ribbon,
A gorilla holding an umbrella,
A caterpillar riding an armadillo
And a chinchilla just chillin'.

Wow! There's a parrot
And a rabbit with a carrot,
I swear it!
A cockatoo just flew
I Out of the locker room,
declare it!

I see a toucan
On the recycling bin!

> Monkeys on the bars?
> You bet there are!
>
> Now I hear a lion
> And I am not lyin'!

> Behind that door
> I hear *ROAR!*
>
> My teacher is petting a tiger,
> I hope it doesn't bite her!
> But it really seems to like her.
> I promise I'm not a liar!
>
> As I stand and stare,
> From out of nowhere
> A frog lands in my hair!
> *PLOP!* Then *HOP!*
> *HOP! HOP! HOP!*
> This is going on my blog!
>
> I hear a hypnotic hip-hop hippopotamus,
> I recognize a riveting rhyming rhinoceros.
>
> Whoa! My cousin Leonard
> Just about lost his freckles
> When he almost got leveled
> By a lively leapin' leopard!
>
> I reach up to wipe my eyes
> When to my great surprise
> My face is grazed
> By the beautiful wings
> Of a big blue butterfly!
>
> I spot the brilliant Clifford Gifford --
> He's the undisputed class math wizard.
> So busy figuring is he
> That he nearly steps on a lizard.
> The look on his face
> Brings more than one snicker.

Ha ha! He He!
Oh my! Oh me!
I can't help but laugh
At that silly giraffe
Who has stuck his neck
Through the basketball net.

There's my friend Patty Byrne
Riding on a pachyderm --
All around the gym
It does carry her.

There's my sister's BFF,
Her name is Lisa --
She can be a bit of a diva.
But it's not easy to be a diva
When you're distracted by a zebra.
And it's even *harder* to be a diva
When you're chased by a cheetah.
Poor diva Lisa!

Oh look! There's my neighbor Sara Snyder.
Oh no! I see a hairy scary spider beside her.

Right now I'm in a dither
And my courage it withers
'Cuz up and down the bleachers
A python it slithers.

What in the --
Here comes Ally Gaither,
Running as fast
As her legs can take her.
What is she saying?
AL -- AL -- ALLI -- GATOR!
Well that does it for me,
I'm outta here,
See ya later!

....

Don't worry about me,
I'm safe in my bed.
But these incredible images
Still play in my head.

I know they seem kookoo
And they even seem scary
But it's really all good
'Cuz it's all imaginary.

When I activate my imagination,
I can create cool creations
And animate awesome animations
Or mutate mutant mutations
And combine creative combinations
Or visualize varieties of variations.
I can narrate nutty narrations,
I can carry on crazy conversations,
I can decide on delightful destinations
And lollygag in loony locations.
Yes! I can visit all kinds of places
And turn all types of pages.
I can command
A rotating claymation space station
Or even defend against
A blazin' invasion of robotic ravens.
I can think ANY story
When it's all imaginary.

If I can only imagine,
I can make ANYTHING happen --
I can be the captain
Of a flashin' rocket wagon.
I can be Aladdin
And live in a magic mansion
With my princess Jasmine
And our pet magic dragon.
I can invent a laser cannon
And all kinds of awesome gadgets.
I can be a legendary luminary
Or veterinary to *Tom and Jerry*,
A scientist in an interplanetary laboratory,
I can even read flying books
In a magical fairy library.
It's no prob', Bob!
After all,
It's all imaginary.

I think you can see
My imagination runs deep --

I need it now
To call those sheep
So I can count them
As they bleat and leap
And play in fields
And on hills so steep.
My eyes feel heavy,
It's off to sleep.

Space

Not a caged lion---Or a fish in a bowl,

Nothing that beautiful----More like a beetle

Pinned to cork----Or a housefly

Beating itself to death.----This open door is not

Wide enough to fly from----This syllable is short

enough----To die from.

Sometimes when I wake up...

...in the middle of the night
i like to look out the window
and see the stars
who are there no matter what
they are there for me
when blood is streaming down the blade
that i use to cut all my feelings away
and they are there
when it is 1:30 a.m. and i am sitting on the floor
drowning in my own tears
and they understand
that when i say i'm tired, or fine,
what i really mean is
help me i'm dying
the stars know
what is going on
the stars know
what is happening
i want to touch the stars
jump out the window
and fly up to them
they will welcome me
comfort me
and i will be safe
i will be safe

That Feeling

I don't want to have a feeling so I close up
like a book or a jacket or a sack which holds
a body. Don't mind me, I'll just be dead in here,
you can drag me wherever you want, the body
seems to say. You laugh like a little silver moon.
You laugh like the moon on the water ignored
by necking lovers. You said you didn't like that word
because something so sweet should not call to mind
giraffes, but I love the word "necking," the way it twists
in on itself, like what I do to you when I want
to disappear in you, leave the sack of my body
strewn on the shore of you. Sometimes I'm inside
the sack and then sometimes I am nothing more
than the stitching which keeps it from bursting.
Sometimes I carry the sack and sometimes the sack
carries me. I only know the difference sometimes.
Do you ever feel like it's difficult to figure out
what you're feeling? I have that all the time, especially
when I look out a window or at your open face.

across from me in bed, or your closed face
when I see the quiet pain you contain, or which
contains you. I know you're more than that
frown which makes your face resemble a fist
with gorgeous black hair. I know you contain more than the
reaction to my words or my body.
Some of us have to learn to love with hands
interlocked, but each with our own hand

In the end

Life is full of questions but fewer answers,
No time to discover everything around us.
We're dropped onto the field of existence,
Surviving among others in the same fight.
The circles we occupy often grow smaller,
Against our intention more often than not.
Because we're forced to move constantly.
And the narrowed space raises our stake.
This process pins us against one another,
While we battle in the fray for a sanctuary.
Our piece of Eden costs the highest price,
Knowing that it leaves us alone in the end

Meek minds and the feeble state quite the opposite
Of course they would make you think it's the weak
None whom proclaim "normality" could fake immunity
Or own the mountainside never reaching the peak
The squanders are those who discard such potential
Only to claim inability or ignorance as their excuse
Notice how quick they recede out from the spotlight
Yet linger at hope to climb in the end.

Tears of the Broken Hearted

Love held out most valiantly
then into the hidden mists perished

Both hope and faith fell as well
along with all we ever cherished

Our selfishness waged a war
we never had any chance to win

Yet every day we closed our eyes
and raised our battle flags again

Once led by the best intentions
long under siege charity retreated

Kindness stood against all odds
though sadly she too was defeated

Just one more try a cry called out
before fallen even peace departed

Until nothing was left but carnage
and the tears of the broken hearted

Inspiration

If I could bottle inspiration,
I imagine it would smell like honeysuckle and tangerines.
Its color would be as green as the grass stains on my favorite jeans and specks of golden sunshine would flash when shaken.
I would drink it every morning and every night when I sat down to write, even though it would taste nothing like how it smelled.
It would be sour and earthy, it would leave a white coat on my tongue, but I would down it every day anyway.
I know why inspiration is the way it is for me.
Each taste, smell, color are a piece of you that I can still feel even though I can no longer touch you.
Because even though you are no longer with me, you are my inspiration

The Deterioration of Bananas

the deterioration of bananas drives me madder than mad
seeing Lola with a calm peaceful spirit gets me high
trying to count money with one hand is hard enough to go insane at times
but, why oh why…oh why do I try
conversations with my mom are tough when we disharmonize
though feelings never leave this blue box of emotions
a box with many shades though some are dark and gloomy
some light up the room leaving us destitute from sunshine
we are here in this world to radiate and shine
to bask like the floweret that revealed its first bud
drinking eight cups of water each day and getting eight hours of sleep
eight is the age that I had my first taste of alcohol
a towel on the floor and a rose perished so 'beautifully'
I wonder with doubt will these new jeans fit properly
The millipede on the wall doesn't bother me at all
I try so often that my brain seems to explode
When family is all you have; and it feels like a circus of clowns
And these people are obscure to me I wonder if I know them at all. Do these folks truly understand how I feel about bananas.
The deterioration of bananas makes me madder than mad.

The Crown

before you go rotten you go sickeningly sweet
no one can kiss you without getting a tooth ache
no one can kiss you without making a mess
lips so ripe they drip onto the floor
blend with the wine splattered rug
and the spilled nail polish
your mother is getting sick of all these stains in the carpet
your father is too afraid to ask where they came from
and it's just as well
because you'd just smile
nothing sugarcoated except your teeth
you're hard to love and you wield it like a weapon
you're easy to leave and you wear it like a crown

McDonald's is Mathematically Impossible

Eating food from McDonald's is mathematically impossible.
Because before you can eat it, you have to order it.
And before you can order it, you have to decide what you want.
And before you can decide what you want, you have to read the menu.
And before you can read the menu, you have to be in front of the menu.
And before you can be in front of the menu, you have to wait in line.
And before you can wait in line, you have to drive to the restaurant.
And before you can drive to the restaurant, you have to get in your car.
And before you can get in your car, you have to put clothes on.
And before you can put clothes on, you have to get out of bed.
And before you can get out of bed, you have to stop being so depressed.
And before you can stop being so depressed, you have to understand what depression is.
And before you can understand what depression is, you have to think clearly.
And before you can think clearly, you have to turn off the TV.
And before you can turn off the TV, you have to free your hands.
And before you can free your hands, you have to stop masturbating.
And before you can stop masturbating, you have to get off.
And before you can get off, you have to imagine someone you really like with his pants off, encouraging you to explore his enlarged genitalia.
And before you can imagine someone you really like with his pants off encouraging you to explore his enlarged genitalia, you have to imagine that person stroking your neck.

And before you can imagine that person stroking your neck, you have to imagine that person walking up to you looking determined.

And before you can imagine that person walking up to you looking determined, you have to choose who that person is.

And before you can choose who that person is, you have to like someone.

And before you can like someone, you have to interact with someone.

And before you can interact with someone, you have to introduce yourself.

And before you can introduce yourself, you have to be in a social situation.

And before you can be in a social situation, you have to be invited to something somehow.

And before you can be invited to something somehow, you have to receive a telephone call from a friend.

And before you can receive a telephone call from a friend, you have to make a reputation for yourself as being sort of fun.

And before you can make a reputation for yourself as being sort of fun, you have to be noticeably fun on several different occasions.

And before you can be noticeably fun on several different occasions, you have to be fun once in the presence of two or more people.

And before you can be fun once in the presence of two or more people, you have to be drunk.

And before you can be drunk, you have to buy alcohol.

And before you can buy alcohol, you have to want your psychological state to be altered.

And before you can want your psychological state to be altered, you have to recognize that your current psychological state is unsatisfactory.

And before you can recognize that your current psychological state is unsatisfactory, you have to grow tired of your lifestyle.

And before you can grow tired of your lifestyle, you have to repeat the same patterns over and over endlessly.

And before you can repeat the same patterns over and over endlessly, you have to lose a lot of your creativity.

And before you can lose a lot of your creativity, you have to stop reading books.

And before you can stop reading books, you have to think that you would benefit from reading less frequently.

And before you can think that you would benefit from reading less frequently, you have to be discouraged by the written word.

And before you can be discouraged by the written word, you have to read something that reinforces your insecurities.

And before you can read something that reinforces your insecurities, you have to have insecurities.

And before you can have insecurities, you have to be awake for part of the day.

And before you can be awake for part of the day, you have to feel motivation to wake up.

And before you can feel motivation to wake up, you have to dream of perfectly synchronized conversations with people you desire to talk to.

And before you can dream of perfectly synchronized conversations with people you desire to talk to, you have to have a general idea of what a perfectly synchronized conversation is.

And before you can have a general idea of what a perfectly synchronized conversation is, you have to watch a lot of movies in which people successfully talk to each other.

And before you can watch a lot of movies in which people successfully talk to each other, you have to have an interest in other people.

And before you can have an interest in other people, you have to have some way of benefiting from other people.

And before you can have some way of benefiting from other people, you have to have goals.

And before you can have goals, you have to want power.

And before you can want power, you have to feel greed.

And before you can feel greed, you have to feel more deserving than others.

And before you can feel more deserving than others, you have to feel a general disgust with the human population.

And before you can feel a general disgust with the human population, you have to be emotionally wounded.

And before you can be emotionally wounded, you have to be treated badly by someone you think you care about while in a naive, vulnerable state.

And before you can be treated badly by someone you think you care about while in a naive, vulnerable state, you have to feel inferior to that person.

And before you can feel inferior to that person, you have to watch him laughing and walking towards his drum kit with his shirt off and the sun all over him.

And before you can watch him laughing and walking towards his drum kit with his shirt off and the sun all over him, you have to go to one of his outdoor shows.

And before you can go to one of his outdoor shows, you have to pretend to know something about music.

And before you can pretend to know something about music, you have to feel embarrassed about your real interests.

And before you can feel embarrassed about your real interests, you have to realize that your interests are different from other people's interests.

And before you can realize that your interests are different from other people's interests, you have to be regularly misunderstood.

And before you can be regularly misunderstood, you have to be almost completely socially debilitated.

And before you can be almost completely socially debilitated, you have to be an outcast.

And before you can be an outcast, you have to be rejected by your entire group of friends.

And before you can be rejected by your entire group of friends, you have to be suffocatingly loyal to your friends.

And before you can be suffocatingly loyal to your friends, you have to be afraid of loss.

And before you can be afraid of loss, you have to lose something of value.

And before you can lose something of value, you have to realize that that thing will never change.

And before you can realize that that thing will never change, you have to have the same conversation with your grandmother forty or fifty times.

And before you can have the same conversation with your grandmother forty or fifty times, you have to have a desire to talk to her and form a meaningful relationship.

And before you can have a desire to talk to her and form a meaningful relationship, you have to love her.

And before you can love her, you have to notice the great tolerance she has for you.

And before you can notice the great tolerance she has for you, you have to break one of her favorite china teacups that her mother gave her and forget to apologize.

And before you can break one of her favorite china teacups that her mother gave her and forget to apologize, you have to insist on using the teacups for your imaginary tea party. And before you can insist on using the teacups for your imaginary tea party, you have to cultivate your imagination.

And before you can cultivate your imagination, you have to spend a lot of time alone.

And before you can spend a lot of time alone, you have to find ways to sneak away from your siblings.

And before you can find ways to sneak away from your siblings, you have to have siblings.

And before you can have siblings, you have to underwhelm your parents.

And before you can underwhelm your parents, you have to be quiet, polite and unnoticeable.

And before you can be quiet, polite and unnoticeable, you have to understand that it is possible to disappoint your parents.

And before you can understand that it is possible to disappoint your parents, you have to be harshly reprimanded.

And before you can be harshly reprimanded, you have to sing loudly at an inappropriate moment.

And before you can sing loudly at an inappropriate moment, you have to be happy.

And before you can be happy, you have to be able to recognize happiness.

And before you can be able to recognize happiness, you have to know distress.

And before you can know distress, you have to be watched by an insufficient babysitter for one week.
And before you can be watched by an insufficient babysitter for one week, you have to vomit on the other, more pleasant babysitter.
And before you can vomit on the other, more pleasant babysitter, you have to be sick.
And before you can be sick, you have to eat something you're allergic to.
And before you can eat something you're allergic to, you have to have allergies.
And before you can have allergies, you have to be born.
And before you can be born, you have to be conceived.
And before you can be conceived, your parents have to copulate.
And before your parents can copulate, they have to be attracted to one another.
And before they can be attracted to one another, they have to have common interests.
And before they can have common interests, they have to talk to each other.
And before they can talk to each other, they have to meet.
And before they can meet, they have to have in-school suspension on the same day.
And before they can have in-school suspension on the same day, they have to get caught sneaking off campus separately.
And before they can get caught sneaking off campus separately, they have to think of somewhere to go.
And before they can think of somewhere to go, they have to be familiar with McDonald's.
And before they can be familiar with McDonald's, they have to eat food from McDonald's.
And eating food from McDonald's is mathematically impossible

She

she cries
she laughs
she runs
she stares
she stares at the walls
she stares at your eyes
she stares at your smile.
she's sad
she's upset
she feels depressed all the time.
please don't let her go

leave her
please help her get up when she falls
please don't ruin anything, especially those walls
please hold her safe and tight.
she just can't stop.
she screams
she cries
she starves
she's broken inside
she has voices in her mind
she is in pain
she still smiles

Spring falls

this smoke gets me high
from the explosion when
our minds collide

this summer was cold
and when it rained
it poured

you were my shelter
when my world was a storm

you made me feel better
when it was cold you were my warmth

I found the answers to my prayers
in the silence
between your
heart beats

Pause

I close my eyes…………To steal time away

From what's real……To pause….My life as it is

And envision…….One…….With you in it.

Never Enough

The way they twist your words into nothing. It doesn't mean anything – nothing does. And it never did. Tomorrow is but an experiment.

Like yesterday never was, forever we chase no matter what, it's never ever enough.

No matter what, it's never enough no it's never ever enough.

Our lives acting like timelines entangled into an uncomfortable knot but it doesn't matter much nothing ever does

Pause, two

I open my eyes……to see the world around me
The beauty within…I pause...and looked at you
And envision.... you and I married, with a child.

Leaves Fall

Leaves fall,
Reminding us,
That things,
Can not be stopped,
From changing,
That we'll,
End up,

Burnt orange,
Decayed,
On the earth's,
Blanketed floor.

So Normal

I stuff my throat,
With your seemingly,
So normal,
And happy.
I don't know how,
You're like this,
But I absolutely,
Love it.
So hungry to be,
Like everyone else,
That it slowly,
Starts eating away,
Nibbling at the teeny,
Tiny pieces of my being.
I just want
Two things,
Out of all this world,
You, and to be a better partner

Butterfly girl

I know a girl
Who is a butterfly
She dances in the rain
And sings lovely with the wind
And plays with the dew
On webs spiders spun
And says a little prayer
Where the grass has thinned
From where
She did her dance too long

I loved a girl
Who was a butterfly
Without saying a word
We said *'goodbye'*
But I see her sometimes
In the big blue sky
Teaching herself how to fly

The Ballet...a Dance

God is in me when I dance.
God, making Spring
While I leap and pirouette
Out of his thoughts
And building worlds
By wishing.
God
Created ballet for many to inspire
For the lead ballerina in Swan Lake
Laughing at his own
Queer fancies,
Standing in awe,
And sobbing;
Musing,
Dreaming,
Amazed in the motion
Perfectly soft arms
Throbbing;
Commanding;
Creating—God's in me when I dance

To a Dancer

Intoxicatingly
Her eyes across the footlights gleam,
(The wine of love, the wine of dream,)
Her eyes, the gleam for me!

The eyes of all that see
Draw to her glances, stealing fire
From her desire that leaps to my desire:
Her eyes that gleam for me!

Subtly, deliciously,
A quickening fire within me, beat
The rhythms of her poising feet;
Her feet that poise to me!

Her body's melody,
In silent waves of wandering sound,
Thrills to the sense of all around,
Yet thrills alone for me!

And O, intoxicatingly,
When, at the magic moment's close,
She dies into the rapture of repose,
Her eyes that gleam for me!

Spheres

So did she move ; so did she sing
Like the harmonious spheres that bring
unto their souls; their music's aid;
Which she performed in such a way,
As all the world will say
The elegant exquisite Vespertine danced, and the grand Apollo
gracefully magnificently played.

I loved you

before we fully knew what loving was.
and god, when we kissed
i could taste the stratosphere unfolding
revealing the suns and moons and constellations

that you kept hidden behind your lips.

When you left

you kissed me goodbye.
you thought you were giving me comfort
or something to hold on to,
but darling
you tasted like tears,
and I felt our future
fall apart in your arms.

I've learned to...

...bottle up my
feelings until
they press
tightly against
glass walls
crack and spill
upon
wooden floors
where we used to
dance to nothing
but your quiet hum
and the steady strumming
of your hearts

my prime objective

will never mean to hurt you/ but I cannot stay silent./Not anymore, no/not while you are hurting me

Exorcism

I can no longer pretend the flowers are enough,
flowers in ink, flowers on plates, flowers in my shoe
laces, candied flowers, 1-800 FLOWERS, balloon,
birthday, funeral flowers, marshmallow flowers staining
the milk pink. Flowers in my mother's scarf that frames her smile
lines grown deep long-term health effects of appearing
gentle in a hostile setting. Have you read the instructions on
tigers?

They may attack the unfamiliar. Remain calm, move slowly,
adapt to the tremor of leaves. To survive is to convince
the predator you are not really there.
I can no longer pretend slowly alive, kneeling in the soil
is enough. A nation of neon plastic straws, machines
on the surface of Mars, reminds its citizens to be patient.
Slowly, when the bill passes, slowly through diversity
training, slowly through handshake and t-shirt and apology
and apology and apology and apology and apology. I take a knife
to the dam, bathing in the leaks. There are teeth
in my laughter. Imagine a life of tectonic distortion: gaping, wet,
magma, colliding with, me over there.
I scream my name in the pool, it is almost enough to hear the
terror

I can be. Remember when discovering fire,
the heat of progress pairs a leather palm with new
ways to eat and be eaten.

Lucifer (and his own Hell)

The train pierces through the blackest night,
its beam reveals misshapen forms within the darkness.
There are ten cars on the train, each with one passenger,
Each passenger has their own story, their own worries, their own misery

The woman walked down the street, heading toward home
A loud noise interrupted the thought of the city,
The woman flew like a dove into the air,
And the driver fled

The man walked out of the bar, heading toward home
Out of the shadows, leaped a foul creature
That wielded a blade. The blade swung, the man fell over,
And the creature fled

The bank cried nervously, streams ran from here to there
A man trampled through the water, stopping the flow
The bank stopped crying, the man took the money.
And he fled

The prisoner glided through the hall, calm as stone
The prisoner glided through the hall, calm as stone
Guards led him toward the courthouse
But he turned and stabbed a guard
And the prisoner fled

The woman kept to herself,
She was always at home, but the neighbors found out
She kept her dead husband with her
And the woman fled

Two hunters walked, through a thick wood
One turned to the other and laughed
He pulled out his gun and fired,
And the hunter fled

A janitor at a stadium, had several interests
One was witchcraft and the other, dead meddling
A guard saw him in the cemetery,
And the janitor fled

Johnny loved guns
Johnny loved guns
He loved them so much
Then he shot a man out on the street
And Johnny fled

A foreigner wanted fame,
But he couldn't find any. So in a rage,
He killed a man
And the foreigner fled

Lucifer loved God,
When God created humans.
Lucifer was angry
Lucifer defied God
Lucifer fled

To my Family...

Poetry is many things. Poetry is life, it is water, it is earth, it is sound, it is music…But most of all, poetry is a language that says, 'Stay alive, do not die on me, do not move away from life.' Because poetry is life, and it keeps people alive.

Constellation

at night i'd look up to the sky
a jet black canvas
and with a paintbrush i would
draw the words stuck in my head
in between the stars
connect them with straight lines
creating constellations
each time a new masterpiece
i'd marvel at them
how could such things come out of a human being?
they couldn't
because my hand wasn't my hand
my voice wasn't my voice
my words weren't my words
a fallen angel
a demon
took over
She was the muse and the creator

beautiful death
i believed
but death is not beautiful
it is not romantic
and i'd rather paint my own sunrise
than watch a murderer
paint the sky with destruction
and in the dark
is where She lives
so give me a new day
early morning
wake me up
I'm waking up
I said my goodbye
now give me a hello

Demons of Darkness

Vespertine stood on the bridge
In silence and fear
For the demons of darkness
Had driven her here

They cut her heart
Right out of her chest
Making her believe
That the demons knew best

They were always there
Sometimes just out of sight
Waiting in the background
Till the time was right

These demons were destructive
Knocking down the life she knew
Hating everything about her
She hated herself too

These demons can't be seen
But they're far from fairy tales
They live inside your mind
Their evilness prevails

So on the bridge she stood
About to end the fight
Then she stopped and thought
I'll fight them one more night

Midnight and the Moths

This is the tale of John Smith.

Mr. Smith was a gentleman, with the respect of everyone in his town. He resided in the town of Little Creek, and his abode was the largest house in the town square. J.Smith was known for throwing immense parties and knowing just about everyone in the town. No one really knows how or when he arrived in Little Creek one can just say that he has always lived there.

Some said that he grew up in the west side of town as a poor boy and changed his name to earn the respect of the people; others said he never aged and he had lived on the square three centuries ago. The real fact was: no one knew John Smith's story.

While everyone knew J.Smith himself, not one person in the town of Little Creek could tell you where he came from, who his family was, or how he got to be so rich. John Smith began to earn himself the title of the "The Great Gatsby" of Little Creek.

Then John Smith disappeared.

It was the night of April 30th, 1967. J.Smith was throwing what is known as his last and most infamous party. The party's fame is not just caused Smith's disappearance, but the discovery of what was living in his basement.

John Smith had a moth farm in his basement. If one were to go downstairs, they would not notice the secret entrance to this strange farm. There was a secret door hidden behind a gun cabinet that led to a long hallway filled with rows of tanks of moths. When authorities finally made a count, there were over three hundred moth tanks. No one in the town knew why.

J.Smith's disappearance was the source of the discovery of his moth farm. It was around 11:28 P.M. and Smith had just finished toasting his guests for coming to his party. Once the toast was over, the behavior of the party returned to normal with guests chatting this way and that, switching conversations with one another every minute or so.

It was at that moment when a guest who drank far too much had stumbled and knocked over an expensive statue of Smith's. The statue rocked to the side and smashed into pieces on the floor. The room fell silent and everyone waited to see what J.Smith would say. After two minutes of waiting, John Smith made no appearance. His guests and employees began to look around the room and see if he was simply not speaking.

"Mr. Smith", one of his servants called out. "There has been an accident in the ballroom!"

There was no response, silence. Three servants left the room quickly in an attempt to find the whereabouts of their missing employer.

Within an hour, Smith was yet to be found. A small search party of guests who were sober enough to look began to split up on various levels of the house to find their host. The guests searched all the rooms on the top floor, main floor, and in the attic. They had yet to search downstairs in the basement.

Due to the size of a basement, not all the guests searching could go down, so a party of ten descended into what appeared to be a private office.

Smith's office was also a private lounge. There was a billiard table in the center of the room, a large sofa to the left and a bookcase filled with hundreds of tales of classic American literature. Next to this bookcase was the gun cabinet. The search party did not find anything, and they reported to the head butler that Mr. Smith was nowhere to be found.

The head butler contacted the authorities, within half an hour, there were two patrol cars parked outside John Smith's home. The police called the party off and all of the guests had to leave. It was fifteen minutes till 2:00 A.M. and the guests should have been home already. The police checked all of the rooms the guests searched through and received the same results. Mr. Smith was not in his house, he had simply disappeared.

That was when an officer found that the appearance of the gun cabinet in Smith's office looked peculiar and he pressed along the back wall of the cabinet. It swung open to reveal a room filled with moth tanks.

The next day there were newspaper reporters, detectives, and officers going in and out of J.Smith's home. Taking pictures here and there but the most were taken of the bizarre discovery within the basement. The police made another discovery in Smith's office that just added more puzzlement to the mystery.

On John Smith's desk there was a note that was scrawled in messy handwriting. It was clearly Smith's and it based on the quality of appearance, it was written in great haste. The words on the note were not in English, nor to this day have they been found to exist in any language. The note read:

Buterflyy डेंज इराउल्जरॉट 1422asd Tod, heute Nacht abliftterun 2:00 暴風雨在一起

The authorities had no idea what they had just read. It was clearly written with the English alphabet, covered up by various languages but the words appeared to be pure gibberish. There were enough questions involved to get the Little Creek's news' attention.

Where did John Smith go? Why did he have a hidden moth farm in his basement? Why were the moths so disturbed fluttering around and killing one another? What does the note on his desk mean? Why are there certain phrases crossed out? Why was the note written with such urgency and in various languages? How could Smith have disappeared so quickly after he gave his toast? Why did no one see him leave the ballroom?

These questions reached national status and the disappearance of John Smith quickly became one of the biggest mysteries of the decade. Professors of Latin, Romanian, Spanish, Greek, Mayan, and Native American history and language were just a few of the hundred that came to Little Creek in an attempt to crack J.Smith's code.

A few other puzzling pieces of evidence were collected from Smith's office. There was an article about the development of ancient Moths in the 19th century, a sketch of a murder scene, and a photograph of a solar eclipse. Despite the level of confusion added from these pieces, none of them could puzzle more than John Smith's note. Or was it his writing on the note after all?

Some say it was a suicide note, others cry foul play and even murder. And, some still think it was some sort of message. Only one word in the message was able to be translated and that was "Butterfly". It was scrawled at the beginning of the note in English. No one is necessarily sure as to why "Butterfly" was written as the first word. Often people propose the idea that the note was a brief letter to his Lord, but that does still not provide an explanation as to why John Smith disappeared.

To this day, the disappearance of John Smith remains one of the greatest mysteries of this little town. Little Creek, Montana had achieved infamous status for a long period of time due to the incident, but eventually the state of Little Creek had dwindled down back to a small town.

John Smith's home is now the only moth museum in history and his basement office is kept in the exact same condition as it was left since the night he disappeared. The office is open for investigators and spectators to view, there are but a few thousand dead moth carcasses in the hidden room, but no further progress has been made on the mystery since the night John Smith was mauled by moths and eaten with such fury… or rather he "disappeared".

The Truths surrounding the utmost exotic childhood snack...Fruit Cocktail.

With its striped triangular "kernels" made of sugar, wax and corn syrup, candy corn was a nostalgic treat, harkening back to days when humans grew, rather than manufactured, food. But what was fruit cocktail's secret meaning? It glistened as though varnished. Faint of taste and watery, it contained anemic grapes, wrinkled and pale. Also deflated maraschino cherries. Fan-shaped pineapple chunks, and squares of bleached peach and pear completed the scene. Fruit cocktail's colorlessness, its lack of connection to anything living, (like tree, seed or leaf) seemed cautionary, sad. A bowl of soupy, faded, funeral fruit. No more nourishing than a child's finger painting, masquerading as happy appetizer, fruit cocktail insisted on pretending everything was ok. Eating it meant you embraced tastelessness. It meant you were easily fooled. It meant you'd pretend semblances

no matter how pathetic they were, and that. When thing got dicey, you'd spurn the truth

Eating fruit cocktail meant you might deny
that ghosts whirled throughout the house
and got sucked up the chimney on nights
Dad wadded old newspapers, warned you
away from the hearth, and finally lit a fire.

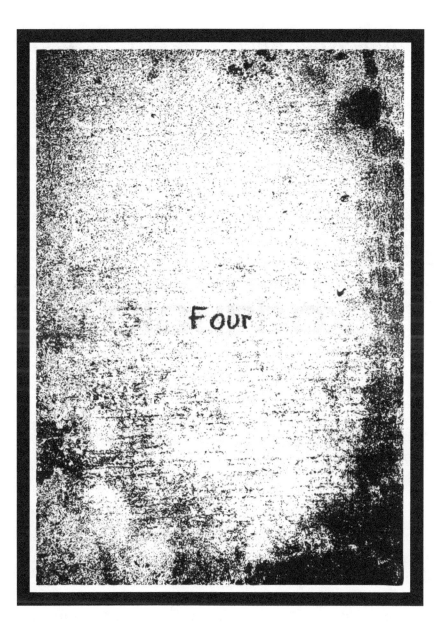

The Gospel according to the Lady Vespertine

I want to be the blade striking
a field of restless people of vanity;

American beauty or the same simple stress, warm branch
of man pinning me here in mute study. To be an ache

in the breast of a burst jelly is what I wanted, vine-slick
and torrid in summer's greed, pressing my fears against

the light of the lonely. Nameless, I haunt for god and love
in extinct places, curve myself inside desire's eye and drink.

All peeled flaming scarlet, all caught promise. Again all
American beauty, and finally.
To be seen. Is what I wanted. To crawl and caress the sleep of his body.

To make a burning room of this home. I seemed eager
a spider bite and the holy grail, a cup of chalice. Stone cold drunken and suppressed quietly,

as life unfolds its sticky tongue in me. Snuffing and whirling me sweetly.

Isn't this love? To walk hand in hand toward the humid dark,
enter the ghost web of the hungry, to consider some wants

were not meant to be understood. Some women are forgiven.
The way my brother prays I'll still find a man to divine me,

and my father tells me lazy women will never be loved.
Like today's new trumpet pushing its bright flower

in my slutty way. The slow voice of its angel hissing breathless:
No. She is not here. He is not here. They are nowhere.

This is the…Gospel according to the Lady Vespertine. **Amen**

If I were a book

If I were a book, I would be torn and tattered.
If I were a toy, I'd be broken and battered.
If I was a mirror, I would be scratched and shattered.
But really, let's face it. None of that matters.
Cause I'm just a man with a brain that's all scattered.

Separate self

I am made of leaving
this dark, dark world
and you are
too
eyes bright
sighing
in our separate selves
untouched
vision is a heartbeat
shooting past the curve of your cheek
knelt at the edge of the white sheet
we observe the fluttering lashes
witness
a corridor of beds
emptying
the gradual absence
walking through
a threshold drawn close
an open door
soon we all fall
to bed
and sleep

Sorry, me

I expect so much from myself, from my mind and my body, that it's only fair to say sorry. Sorry for complaining about being tired, without having rested properly. Sorry for overloading my mind with things and expecting to do everything perfectly. Sorry for forgetting that I am not a machine and I can break down. I am always careful not to hurt everyone's feelings but I never consider that I also need to apologize to myself for everything I put me through.

Sorry, me (part two)

What drives me is to be able to lecture myself when I need to be lectured and to motivate my emotions, my sorry's, myself, when I need to be motivated. Growth, the very ritual of admittance and all that it entails, living in the present tense, experiencing things for how they personally feel rather for how they are or for how the rest of the world paints them out to be. Apologies, cultivation of one's heart; it all starts from the inside of a person. It all starts from how unique and empowered and singular a person can feel within themselves.

Your heart; my soul

Been chasing your mind
Running after your heart
Searching your fingertips
for my soul in the dark

Sippin' Vodka

A new priest at his first mass was so nervous he could hardly speak.

After mass he asked the monsignor how he had done.

The monsignor replied, 'When I am worried about getting nervous On the pulpit, I put a glass of vodka next to the water glass. If I start to get nervous, I take a sip.'

So next Sunday he took the monsignor's advice.

At the beginning of the sermon, he got nervous and took a drink…and

He proceeded to talk up a storm.

Upon his return to his office after the mass, he found the following note on the door:

1) Sip the vodka, don't gulp.

2) There are 10 commandments, not 12.

3) There are 12 disciples, not 10.

4) Jesus was consecrated, not constipated.

5) Jacob wagered his donkey, he did not bet his ass.

6) We do not refer to Jesus Christ as the late J.C.

7) The Father, Son, and Holy Ghost are not referred to as Daddy, Junior and Casper.

8) David slew Goliath, he did not kick the sh*t out of him.

9) When David was hit by a rock and was knocked off his donkey, don't say he was stoned off his ass.

10) We do Not refer to the cross as the 'Big T.'

11) When Jesus broke the bread at the last supper he said, 'take this and eat it for it is my body.' He did not say ' Eat me'

12) The Virgin Mary is not called ' Mary with the Cherry'.

13) The recommended grace before a meal is not: Rub-A-Dub-Dub thanks for the grub, Yeah God.

14) Next Sunday there will be a taffy pulling contest at St. Peter's not a peter pulling contest at St. Taffy's.

Crickets

The lady and dog have gone to bed.
I sit here with the front door open.

Crickets sing patiently, a high pitched croon
in lazy harmony. Rain is falling

on the rooftop; taps of existence,
start and stop. I come back to Earth

into my body. Return to the light. You've
been out fighting bullies and rascals

and pests. You've been talking
to yourself for too many years.

You've been cheering for a family
that doesn't exist. We're all walking on bones.

Some of us are walking on more bones
than others. Breathe. Come back to thee,

little one. The human world is a sunken mess,
but so beautifully corrupt I feel. I dig in my soul

never showing scars; when you don't resist,
no wounds exist. Come, see the light, bring it back; come back.

In this world, we live in bodies of flesh.
In this world our minds shackle themselves

In this world, our families don't much care
how we've come to live in darkness

Never underestimate the powers that be.
tuck in your lady, give the dog a bone

Let the crickets tell you their truth.
Let it be yours, for now. Don't make a sound.

Mask

This is the time where
I separate myself from the rest of the world
in order to hear my own thoughts.
It's a lot easier to be away from people,
No one bothering me,
Not having to fake a smile,
And I can finally take off the mask
I've been hiding in.
I just want to be at peace
knowing that if I'm not around anyone,
they can't judge me… right?

Love, Psycho and Everything in Between

I love you like ladybugs love windowsills, love you
like sperm whales love squid. There's no depth
I wouldn't follow you through. I love you like
the pawns in chess love aristocratic horses.
I'll throw myself in front of a bishop or a queen
for you, even a sentient castle. My love is crazy
like that. Stupid like that. Psycho. I like that sweet little button nose
you have. And your pearly red chapped lips under your snout.
I like to kiss you with my lips to yours, with my tongue all over your tongue,
with gusto, and of course with socks still on and a gaze in my eyes.
 I love you like a vulture loves the careless deer at the side of the road. I want to get
all up in you. With my skin caressing your skin.
I want to lotion your tears and dryness away.
I love you like Morpheus loved Trinity and Neo, Like Luke loved his sister
And Norman loved his mom. And beyond the love
Miss Monroe devoted to her Kennedy.
But her devotion came up a few inches short.
I would train my thirst and learn to be sober until
I retrieved every lost blood vessel I've drowned for you. I swear
this love is ungodly, not an ounce of suffering in it.
Like salmon and its upstream itch, I'll dodge grizzlies for you.

Like bluebirds and redbirds even tiny fluttering hummingbirds
and skyscraper rooftops, and AA meetings I attend every night.
I'll keep coming back. Maddened. A little hopeless.
Embarrassingly in love. Crazy in love. Psycho.
And that's why I'm on the couch kissing pictures on my phone
instead of calling you in from the kitchen where you are…
undoubtedly making dinner way too spicy for me, but when
you hold the spoon to my lips and ask if it's ready
I'll say it is, always, but never, never is there enough
flavor in your chili to compare. Compare me to you.
Our love to one another's fly's high in the sky
 Because you are my ice cream to your hot fudge,
my cranberries to your lindenberries, pork tenderloin to my prime
rib.
I can eat you all up and spit sweet loving air bubbles
that travel beyond the skyscrapers in Hong Kong, Japan.
I love you like that. Freakishly in love. Abundance of love.
I endure your every breath you take and don't take.
Passionately in love. Again I repeat to myself…
"Self", you are freakishly in love.

Undertaker

"I am my heart's undertaker. Daily I go and retrieve its tattered remains, place them delicately into its little coffin, and bury it in the depths of my memory, only to have to do it all again tomorrow."

The Funeral in my Heart

Loneliness is having a party
in my mind again and that's okay.

I am surrounded
by souls.

Some treat me like
sunlight and some treat me like
moonlight.

I cry myself to sleep
and no one knows that the truth
about loneliness is that it protects
ones heart from everything but itself.

There's a funeral in my heart,
and the casket is too small for my
childish soul that screams 'Let me out!'

I want to live without thinking
about who will miss me when I'm gone
because I'm tired of writing all these goodbye
letters that mean nothing without a recipient.

There's a funeral in my heart
and there are no flowers because
nobody wants to give flowers to a suicide.

I wish I can say sorry for being
so selfish but that would mean apologizing
for the nights I've tried to hold it all together
like rebuilding Rome for a day—I have nothing to say.

There's a funeral in my heart
and I am all alone here with the lights closed
because the window might glow and I am not light.

I am not light.

Broken

It surprises me
How truly, madly, deeply
Broken
I am
A speck
Of a dandelion
Blown in the wind
Never to come back again.

A page
Out of a story
Leaving behind…a hole in the plot
A clock
Ticking away
With a fractured hand

Lost in time.
A frame
With a stolen
Picture of a smile
Impossible to replicate.
A heart
Still rhythmic inside
The body
Of a person long expired.

                                        Truly, madly, deeply
                                                      Broken
                                        But still breathing
                                    Still standing upright.
                                                It surprises me

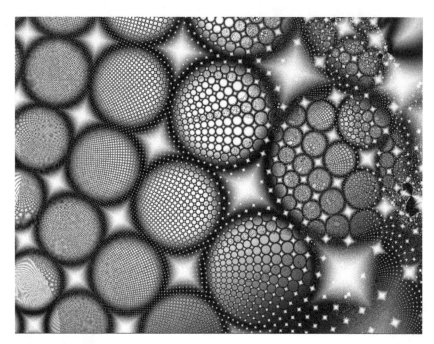

Design 101

Paint me a fresh new beautiful day

And breathe in all these luscious colors

Maintain the purest of wistful skies

That man is sure to discover

The chill of white lace over her thigh

In silken touches of snow

A sparkle of luster shines through the glass

Soft whispers heard from below

"I am fond of you my dear" he states

        "I too, my friend, my companion, my love"

        "You are completely what my soul desires"

"I"...
"Love"...
"You" ...
Fondness is pure and simple like pedals
Although the meaning of love has power
To make the breeze attain its coolness
And the warmth of a simmering summer fire
This beautiful day has meaning for two
And brought together a moment of bliss
The purest of colors seen through one's eyes

In the painting of violets and roses, reminisce.

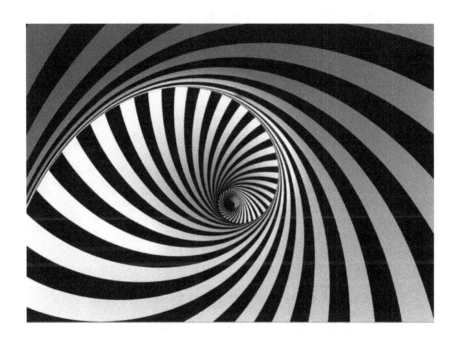

Depression

Maybe if my leg was broken or I was diagnosed with a life-threatening illness they would have cared more. It seems that mental illness does not have a place in this world. There are already too many 'freaks' suffering from it; one in five Australians. in fact. Sure the physical symptoms of depression may not kill me, but the emotional ones may. I know that I can be stronger and fight my depression - I want an education and a career, I never wanted to be a dropout. Finding the motivation to brush my teeth is a struggle, so you can imagine the pain I feel when people called me a faker. The inner sadness that engulfs me is phenomenal. I wouldn't wish it upon my worst enemy. Yet, I would like to see some of the people who ridiculed me go through a fraction of what I have been through for a second and see how they would fight it.

I, like everybody else, have had problems in my life. My parents separating when I was young. I was followed home from school one day and jumped, just because some girls didn't like me. I've suffered the usual bitchiness and name-calling. The saying "sticks and stones may break my bones but words will never hurt me" is so wrong. Being called a 'whore' or 'slut' while still being a virgin has left emotional scars that feel like they will be with me forever. A simple threat sends me into a hysterical state. While physical scars heal, emotional ones are left there to haunt you for the rest of your life. Some people I have considered my 'best friends' have betrayed me. Many haven't called the whole time I have been sick. I'm forgotten now.

I'm extremely lucky to have a caring and understanding family as well as a boyfriend who would do anything to see me happy. I love them all so much. Unfortunately, you hurt the ones you love most. Your pain becomes directed at them and they take the blame for all the shit the world has dealt out to you. I never wanted to hurt them. I hope they can forgive me.

This was written during the darkest times of my depression. Three suicide attempts followed and my family helped me through them. I am now a happy fifty-year-old doing this writing. Upon reflection, the period that I suffered from my depression seems like a bad nightmare. I still can't believe what I went through and survived. There is always hope, for anyone. There is always someone there to listen.

·

de·pres·sion
/dəˈpreSH(ə)n/

Noun

feelings of severe despondency and dejection.
"self-doubt creeps in and that swiftly turns to depression"

The End

Hello,

Do you remember me?

My voice? My smile?

Do you think of me?

Of us? Our memories?

In every waking moment, you haunt me

I have had enough

Like a demon I exorcise you

You are not welcome in my head nor do I want you there

This you know but you stay

Despite how many priests or baptisms

You stay

I am a poor soul held by the chain that is you

Imprisoned by my own mind

Fueled by my own thoughts

At a leisurely pace, my resentment towards you grows into confusion

Was this meant to happen

Is this burden I carry a blessing in disguise. Should I feel this way

I smile weakly and tell the priest I am healed

That I am rid of you

For it is not the action of others that will heal me

But those of myself

I wake up the next morning

Unchained, Untied, Unconfided

Liberated

We Die

Love is Reminding us,
That things,
Can't be stopped,
From changing,
That we'll,
End up,
Burnt orange,
Decayed,
On the earth's,
Blanketed floor
Reminding us,
That things,
Can't be stopped,
From changing,
That we'll,
End up,
Burnt orange,
Decayed,
On the earth's,
Blanketed floor

We Mourn

We mourn, but we are blessed,
we squawk, we wail, we
wind down, we sip,
we spin, we blind, we
bend, bow & look up. We
hip, we blend, we bind,
we shake, we shine,
shine. We lips & we
teeth, we praise & protest.
We document & we
drama. We demand &
we flow, fold & hang. We measure &
we moan, mourn & whine
low. & we live, and we
breathe. & some of the time,
we don't.
Tonight, I am here. Here
& tired. Here & awake,
sure, & alive. Yes here &
still, still here, still & here
& still awake & still still
alive. We mourn.

I think I'm dying

or just killing a part of myself

that I've been trying to kill

for ages and ages...

I think the world around me is

trying to just...forget me...

The people I care about...don't care...

When I try to ask for help in the

few places I feel welcome.. I get put

into a place where I can't ask for the help I
need.

I get investigated and reported for breaking the law of words, and for what? The word "suicide" OMG hide!!!!!

I can't just...call for help...when I'm dying...

Dying is a welcome change, you know,

since it's something new, for once.

I saw a picture that I made my phone background,

my profile picture on basically everything,

and its simplistic nature is what speaks to me.

It's a black figure, submerged in a pool of water,

a set of planets floating above.

It makes me think of what I've lost, and how I feel…

Dying is what I take away from this picture,

escape from the loud life and into a quiet place.

Dying is like being submerged in a pool, floating

down to the bottom like a rock.

Dying is like hiking in a forest far away,

the only sound being your dying thoughts…

I'm looking into the distance, towards the

mountains, knowing it's a dream but

knowing it felt so real…

Learning to warm cold, dead hands is hard,

especially when they're your own…

Bank Account

"Unless you're influenced by my uniqueness, I'm not going to be influenced by your advice. So if you want to be really effective in the habit of interpersonal communication, you cannot do it with technique alone. You have to build the skills of empathetic listening on a base of character that inspires openness and trust. And you have to build the Emotional Bank Accounts that create a connection between hearts.""

Crown me with Flowers

Crown me with flowers, the queen of
redemption, the queen of new days
dawning. I grip hope like a lifeline curling
in and out of time. An eternal anchor
to that which I love, which I love alone.
Queen of the underworld, of cold
and of gray. I live to serve another way.
Through the shadows of doubt I become
unborn, unbent, and unbroken - rising like
Venus from the seas. Birthed from a shell
crafted from wonder and light. Reminiscent
of the moon versus the sun
we coil around each other in the midst
of endless days and nights, freefalling
and born again in the image of our creator.
Say my name and I'll be called to you
summoned past cosmic boarders to stand at
your side through the end of days. The Queen of
redemption, the Queen of spite rendered
sacred, of springs new found and past -

Touching Stars

Sometimes
when i wake up
in the middle of the night
i like to look out the window
and see the stars
That are devotedly and truly there on time
they are there for me and the world to see
when blood is streaming down the blade
that i use to cut all my feelings away
when it's 1:30 a.m. and I'm sitting on the floor
drowning in my own tears
and they understand me
that when i say i'm tired, or fine,
what i really mean is
help me, i'm dying
the stars know
what is going on
the stars know
what is happening
i want to touch the stars
jump out the window
and fly up to them
they will welcome me
comfort me
and i will be safe from all my dilemmas
i will be safe and depressed

(to Dad)

August

In the air
she can
breathe
so thoroughly and passionately,
without another
mortal's soul nearby.

i am a shadow
over broken
glass
on surface
like skin
that taught itself
to heal too much.

on the 14th of this month
they will tell my father
"It's alright, you're doing well,
this room will be much more comfortable."
And from that moment on he will watch his time expire

and somewhere in
this world
someone will
catch a moment
where a yellow flower
braces itself against the snow
in the summer month of August
and flourish…..In the air

Goodbye, Y'all

at night I'd look up to the sky
a jet-black canvas
and with a paintbrush I would
draw the words stuck in my head
in between the stars
connect them with straight lines
creating constellations
each time a new masterpiece
I'd marvel at them
how could such things come out of a human being?
they couldn't
because my hand wasn't my hand
my voice wasn't my voice
my words weren't my words
a fallen angel
a demon
took over

She was the muse and the creator
beautiful death
I believed
but death is not beautiful
it is not romantic
and I'd rather paint my own sunrise
then watch a murderer
paint the sky with destruction
and in the dark
is where She lives
so give me a new day
early morning
wake me up
I'm waking up
i said my goodbye
now give me a hello

must be said. must be read.

(Part Three): "The Wise Ones"

You probably know by now that the world of light is our true home and something like a veil of consciousness separates that sphere of life from ours. The wisdom of our Wise Ones provides that after every period of Earth's tests and trials there comes a time of recuperation. After resting and recovering for a while, another resurrection is always in store for us. If our Karma does not allow for this to take place on this side of the veil of consciousness that separates our two worlds, it is sure to follow on the other side and once again we shall feel joyous and happy.

After a while there comes the moment when we, together with the Wise Ones in charge of us, assess the spiritual progress we have made up to that point. This enables us to see for ourselves that our suffering has made us into a better person with a much-improved understanding of life, as well as a good measure of kindness and compassion, love and wisdom towards our own suffering and that of others. We no longer find it hard to understand that such joyous and precious possessions cannot possibly drop into anyone's lap and come on their own but have to be worked for very hard and earned through past difficulties patiently endured.

Any wisdom that is gained during one of our lifetimes on this Planet Earth, accompanies us into all future ones, where it stands us in good stead and eases our pathway through life. The more highly evolved we become, each time something unpleasant comes our way, our small earthly self takes comfort from saying to itself: 'I know that this is happening for a good and wise reason. It's the Universe's way of helping me to grow ever more God-like and heaven-tall.' And that enables us to smile through our tears.

Who would be wise enough to decide whether joy is a more valuable gift than sorrow? But maybe in truth sorrow is the more precious one. Who can say? Whatever our preference is, the two cannot be separated from each other and are constantly close to us, because both are necessary for leading a full life, in which something can be learnt from every experience and our consciousness expands in wisdom and understanding. Wise Ones, while on the Earth, have come to terms with the fact that joy and sorrow are twins, and that when they are enjoying the presence of one, its sibling is waiting in the wings. They accept that they cannot change being like scales that are constantly tipping to and fro, from joy to sorrow, from the Heavens down to the Earth.

These Wise Ones know that if it were possible to empty ourselves of all feelings, we would be balanced, at peace and in a state of equilibrium at all times. But they are also aware that the world of feelings is the realm of our soul and that that which emerges from there into our conscious awareness is denied and suppressed to our detriment. They are wise because they know from their own experiences what happens when the world of our feelings is treated in this way. Ever deepening depressions are the result, during this lifetime and coming ones. We come down with mysterious illnesses which no-one can identify and knows how to treat effectively. The medical profession is clueless and gives them long and interesting sounding Latin names, as if this in itself were a cure and could bring relief to their patient's distress.

Drugs are prescribed and handed out to the sufferers, which are provided by pharmaceutical companies. They are smiling all the way to the bank, because of the vast profits they are making. Humankind's sorrow and suffering is their joy and delight. Oh, how short-sighted can anyone get! Naturally, those in charge of the suppliers are responsible for their actions, the same as everybody else. Unaware that the exploitation of people's misery for their personal gains is creating ever more negative Karma for themselves and their companies, they continue to happily walk down this slippery slope. The same approach was tried in recent years with the Bird Flu, the Swine Flu and the Ebola outbreak, but thanks to humankind's increasing public awareness, the companies involved in the manufacturing of the 'antidotes' did not succeed.

(to be continued...)

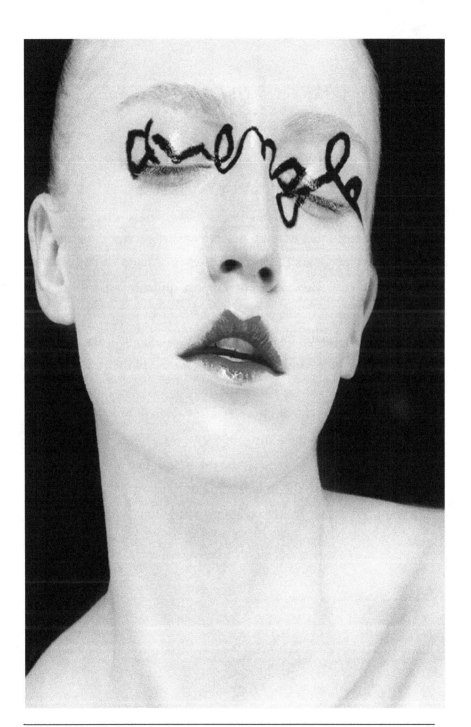

An act of Kindness

Show love so others recognize they're loved.
Kind words always use, in hopes
someone passes them along.
In this world you have to stay strong.
An act of kindness always provide,
with a dash of support applied.
Give a smile to a sad face.
Maybe their sadness you can replace.
Think of others before yourself in just
the small things.
Someone feeling as if he/she doesn't belong
Tell them how their ever so wrong.
Let the elderly be the first in line.
Give the lonely some of your time.
Lend a helping hand to whom is struggling to carry their
groceries in.

Some are homeless living on the street,
cold winters days, buy him/her a warm drink.
Any act of love/kindness you can think.
Be a friend to someone who doesn't have one.
Hold the door open for someone sometime.
For your intentions are to help the world be a better place.
Its no competition, we're not in a race.
Believing one act of kindness truly leads to another.
For we were all born to help each other.

Taste

My lips have always craved the taste of danger.
Maybe it is because I don't know what's good for me
or I'm in love with the high I get from it
The high that takes me to the heavens,
surpassing the pillow-like clouds
resting against the azure canvas
I remember the taste so vividly,
I salivate at the thought of it
It's sweet like candy,
the sugary goodness

rushing inside my veins
delicately coating my tongue
bites between my teeth
explode into a thousand little pieces,
dancing inside my mouth
Your succulent lips pressed against mine,
remind me of the taste of summer strawberries,
juicy and tender with citrusy undertones
we're kissing like there's no tomorrow
Oh how I feel your lips part from mine, then touch
and part again the way the clouds greet the sky
Before a rainy afternoon

How can something so bad taste this good?
Oh I'm convinced your kisses are a drug
Nice to play with, but toxic to the mind
Kissing you must be equivalent to intoxication
shockwaves through my body,
the paralyzing euphoria
I don't think I could ever give you up
This addiction is taking control

Cold Dark Corner

There's a cold dark corner
in the back of my room,
it speaks to me
and says I'm coming for you.

As I lie on my bed
in the fetal position,
my eyes are closed
hoping and wishing.

Maybe that one day
my dreams will come true,
that I don't have to be here
so down and blue.

The corner keeps talking
about how I'm going to die,
all I can do
is lie there and cry.

As the corner gets closer
and takes me in,
my soul starts to burn
as so does my skin.

My bones shall lie there
turning to dust,
my bed surrounding
nothing but rust.

A letter to myself

Dear Self,

I know how you're feeling, but it sounds like we think a bit differently. Yes, there are times where I wish I could've done things differently or maybe not done something at all, but at the same time, I also believe everything happens for a reason.

You cannot change the past. We need to stop thinking of "what if" thoughts in our life because those thoughts are what keep us from moving on. You won't grow as a person if you're stuck in the past. If you're reflecting on the past then use it as a source. Something you should use to think of where you were and where you are now. Become a better person. Become a better you. That is the only time I believe we should reflect back on ourselves.

Don't regret the things you do. Regret the things you don't do. Whether it goes the way you wanted it to or not, it'll either make you stronger or make you more hopeful. You'll be okay no matter the situation. You're stronger than you think. And I promise things get better over time.

Love always,
Self

KEEP SMILING...

BECAUSE YOU'RE BEAUTIFUL!!!

Letter to myself #2

Dear self,

First off, let me start by saying that it's okay to feel like you aren't doing as well as you are supposed to. So if you need to take a second to breathe, to cry, to put your head down, stare out a window or go for a walk. Do that, without distractions. Thank God for everything that you are fortuned with, take a look at all the beautiful things around you, and be stress free for just a moment.

Figure out what you can change, and what you cannot. Most importantly, accept what you cannot change. Become at peace with it, even if just for a brief moment. Say a prayer for your restless heart to be comforted knowing that God is with you in all things. Don't forget to thank Him again. Endless gratitude will take you far.

When you decide that you are ready to face the things that you can change, do it with 100% commitment. That doesn't mean 100% perfection. Start by making a plan. Write it down in a planner, memorize it, put it on a Post-It on the mirror, do whatever makes it the easiest for you. Think through your plan logically, take into consideration your strengths and weaknesses. Remember to do the hard things first once in a while - the relief is sweet in the end. Make a checklist, use an App, tell your best friend about it so they can keep you accountable too. You are ready. You are young. You are smart. You are beautiful

Love Always,
Self

Down to Earth

Found on Earth
A ground on Earth
Bound to Earth --
World of birth
World of worth?
Why my birth
On this Earth?
A bandit planet
A manic planet
Planet of panic
Need some bandage --
Somehow I fell
Into a Hell
A special Hell
For a spell --
The Milky Way
Where I stay
So far away
From the home
Where I belong
This feels wrong
I feel alone --
Low on chances
How many chances
Will be granted?

To be candid
I feel stranded
Hopelessly abandoned
Even empty-handed --
Day to day
(As they say)
A fated castaway --
Must break away
To a brighter day
Light of day --
My feet planted
On this planet
Marked and branded
Was it random?
Is it phantom?
Here I landed
Why here landed?
God planned it --
A new understanding
Consciousness expanded
A better handle
A brighter candle --
Down to Earth?
Up to North
North of Earth --
I stand up
And look up
For backup – in this lovely day.

Eddie

Dreams of darling cherubs so sweet
nightmares of eerie demons from deep
toys and trinkets the feeling of joy
words and punches from some crummy boy
adding and subtraction the beginning of math
the girl I sit next to I must take a bath
golden glorious and shiny is her hair
a beat down from Eddie her boyfriend not fair
coat so ripped and torn in my locker
their attitude so rude I can't hear their banter
my fist his face my blood drips so red
this tragic dilemma I wish I was dead
parents don't notice the bruises I see
God take me away I wish I was free

Black Box

black box – dark hole

I see my mind take control

It has so much relinquishment that insufficient light detects

why I ask preeminent though to muster sighs of thoughtlessness

it cracks it's rupture beyond fixation some might call preposterous

I am of gray, you are of soft, we are of light geriatric gross

black box – hole seen through

my mind looks over to offer you

a thought that might regret self condemnation in this sphere of immature madness

here my stance is poised of carriage but my artillery is just a luscious vanilla

I am of image, you are of eye, we are the wreckless formation of my genius that can mutter a strenuous urge and sigh

black box – warm hole

you see me now undoubtedly out of control

black box – black soul

Parallel

Imagine a Person
just like you
living parallel to you
their life a parallel line to yours
a Person who finds the same thrills as you
loves nothing more than your favorite piece of art
your passions exactly the same
living your life
singing your songs
loving your paintings
a Person so uncannily made for you
someone that you would instantly click with

                 someone that would watch sunsets with you
    someone you would never let go of till the day they die.
         someone quite impossible to deal with at times
         because you just never quite meet in the middle
someone you'll miss by some unusual circumstance
                    and you'll always miss them
         because you see the thing about parallel lines
                       and the story ends
                      Goodbye my friend

A Conversation with Depression

Who are you?

"Well if I knew you would too."

Aren't you my reflection?
Why do you seem like a stranger?

"Well that's the conventional conception
That I am supposed to be you and vice versa,
but of course that doesn't apply to our personas"

I suppose you're right
I fight and cage you.
I'll put Rage outside the door
find anything more to lock you up with.

"Yet here I am.
Slipping through the cracks,
and putting chips in your act.
I'll escape when you're alone
I've done it before and will do it some more."

Well stop it!
Quit bringing your buddies,
Regret and Sadness and whomever else.
I hate you
Why else do I try to kill you?

"You don't hate me,
you're afraid of what I could be.

I get friends as well, you know.
Who cares if they weigh you down?
I don't, so deal with it.
Its what I do with your infuriating companions.

You can't kill me though.
See, if I die you will as well

and I can't fathom you attempting suicide
So just let me inside."

I can't cave in and embrace you
I do that and I'll erase myself.
You don't care about anything
not me or my family
or even yourself
You're a disgrace
to me and the human race.

"So, if I'm a disgrace,
does that make you a saint?

"Please, we both know you aren't
So get off your high horse
I'll agree I don't care how anyone fares
but that's my motto
'No cares and buckets of pain'
So there you go
I'm going to go kick your door down now.
Ciao!"

Already Dead

I'm "already dead."
Believe me, I know.
I'm holding on by a thread,
Just not letting it show.

I learned from the best
How to hide what I feel.
I'm sure I passed the test
Of learning how to deal

But that was before
My heart was torn in half.
I don't care anymore
About faking a laugh.

The blade feels amazing
Against my pale skin.
It started with me grazing,
Then I slid it deeper in.

The steel is biting cold
Against my warm flesh.
But, for now I'm in control,
This feeling is the best.
The blood that's falling
Is torture's sweetest form.
I hear Lucifer calling,
The calm before the storm

The blade knocks against bone,
I hear the shriek of agony.
I know I'm home alone,
Then realize it belongs to me.

I push it in deeper still,
Until I feel it hit my soul.
As good as any pill,
It sends my body cold.

The demons watching closely.,
My family, women, men, friends and foes.
Can finally stop waiting,
For I have returned home.

Wake up, Mommy

My tummy hurts really bad. I tried to tell Mommy, but she was sleeping on the mattress in the living room, she took some pills when she went to bed a couple nights ago. Mommy says they are to make her feel better.

Mommy is always sad. I asked her once, about why she is always sad. Mommy just ruffled my hair though and told me not to worry about Mommy business, but I think she is sad because Daddy hurts Mommy.

Daddy comes home every so often and when he does, he always smells funny. Like that strange man that Daddy told me was my Uncle Brandon. Daddy really hurt Mommy that one time I accidentally spilt Daddy's bag of white stuff on the floor.

Daddy was really angry and scary. He called me the nasty words Mommy tells me not to say and raised his hand. I thought he was going to hurt me like he hurts Mommy, but Mommy stepped in front of me.

I remember crying as Daddy hit Mommy, Mommy was crying too. I thought he would leave her alone after that, but Daddy called Uncle Brandon into the room and told me to get out so 'he could show this bitch who the man of the house was'.

I stayed near the room they were in and heard Mommy screaming, and Daddy laughing while Uncle Brandon was grunting like he was lifting something heavy. They stayed in there for a long time before Daddy stepped out with Uncle Brandon.

My stomach gave another rumble, as I walked to the fridge and opened it. Sighing in disappointment, I closed the fridge. It was empty anyway, Mommy usually went out late at night to get groceries, but she usually doesn't come back until really early in the morning. Walking to Mommy I tried shaking her awake again. She is really cold. I grabbed my blankie and stuffed kitty and went back in the living room. I put the blankie around Mommy and lay beside her with my kitty. I hope Mommy wakes up soon, my tummy really really hurts now.

Author Notes: Abuse is not to be taken lightly, if you or someone you know is being abused, please tell authorities or a trusted adult.

The most glorious dream

I picture myself center stage in the most enormous and beautiful theater in the world. Its walls and ceilings are covered in impeccable Victorian paintings of angels in the sky. A single ray of light shines down upon my face, shining through the still, silent darkness, and all attention is on me and me alone for I want to be cast as the "Leading Player". The theater is a packed house; however, my audience is not that of human beings, but rather the angels from the paintings on the walls come alive, sitting intently in the rows of plush seats. Their warmth encompasses my body, and I know at that moment that it is time to begin.

I open my mouth. From deep inside my soul a melody flows out of my chest, off my tongue, and finally caresses my lips with the sweetest touch, and my song fills the air with a boldness like that of the glory of the angels. The sound of my song is that of unfathomable wonder, a voice as sweet and smooth as the face of a child. I sing and sing and sing my heart out of the opening song of the musical "Pippen". And, I wonder and wonder and wonder in awe of the sound that is coming from my mouth and my throat and my soul, and I sing with more power than I have ever felt before. It takes over my entire body and the adrenaline surges like I never imagined it could surge. My whole world is aglow.

For those precious moments, everything is right, and then I am alone. The angels have disappeared, yet the stage is still mine, and suddenly, from out of nowhere, a piano begins to play. I can't see it, but I can feel it in every cell of my body, and my voice again takes charge and rushes out to court the empty notes of the piano. The two become one, and never before have the theater's walls heard such awesome music. In this enormous theater, I am alone But worthy to have at least fifty chorus and dance members on each side of me, but I have never felt so fulfilled in my life. I look out to the very last row of empty seats, but there appears a man and two ladies. A moment of shock and fear is quickly overridden by a quieting peacefulness. The piano stops playing, leaving my voice the only noise in the arena.

The melody I sing slows down to a to the calm ballad "Corner of the sky" that I sing wholeheartedly for the man and two ladies, all the while with a locked gaze into the man's eyes. His eyes are a mirror. They show me myself. They show me my talent—my beauty on the inside that I never allow myself to see. He shows me who I am meant to be. The ballad ends. There is silence, but a continuous locking of eyes shift to the director who has beautiful large brown piercing eyes. They are the most beautiful eyes I have ever seen—more beautiful than in my dreams. The silence continues, and my feeling of peace continues, until finally I say, "Yes, I understand."

In an instance they are gone to discuss today's audition. . I take one last minute to breathe in the emptiness of the stage and to imprint the experience in my mind where it will stay forever like a fountain from which I will draw happiness. Then I pull myself back into reality. I walk off of the stage, down the steps, through the empty audience, and out the back door of the theater which has changed my life. I walk outside into the new world that has been created for me!

(to Mom)

Divine Peace

May Divine peace fill your whole being,
within and without, today and forever.

May you be able to love and accept yourself,
just the way you are.

May you trust that you are always in the right place.

May you be aware of the infinite possibilities that
have their origin in trusting the basic goodness of your existence
and its Creator, the Great White Spirit, Father/Mother of all life,
who constantly provides for all of everyone's needs,
including yours.

May you use the gifts the Universe has bestowed upon you
for doing your share of making our world into
a more beautiful and peaceful place
for everything that shares it with us. May you be able to give the
full measure of the love
that is the most important part of your being,

to everything that comes your way.

May your soul enjoy the freedom of singing and dancing,
Praising and loving whatever comes your way,
every moment of each day and week, month and year
of your present lifetime
and whatever waits for you beyond. And may God and the Angels
bless you and keep you safe,
now and forever.

Amen

(Part Four): The Wise Ones

Imagine how great the sorrow of the guilty ones will be when their Karma comes to meet and shake hands with them in future lifetimes. How will they react when their suffering is exploited by groups of contemporaries, who are then fulfilling their selfish desires of greed and avarice, they way the guilty ones are doing, now? Love is the law of life and powerful Karmic chains are created by any kind of transgression against this law. However, all is not lost. As soon as the lesson in question has been sufficiently understood by those involved, the Universe in its great wisdom lays the power for dissolving such bonds into everybody's own hands.

The only tool required for setting each other free is forgiveness, first for ourselves for once having set the wheels of Karma in motion, and then for those who have trespassed against us. Forgiveness alone can release us from the obligations towards each other. When this has been duly attended to, there will be no need for repeating the unpleasant experiences. This is our joy, for at last we are free to move on to lessons of a more elevated nature like. The first one is serving as a channel, through which the blessing and healing power of the Lord, the Universal Christ flows into our race's consciousness, and that in both worlds.

And so, next time your soul comes knocking on the inner door of your consciousness, make an effort to listen to what it has to say and invite it in. What it almost certainly is trying to tell you that the time has come for you, its earthly self, to wake from your spiritual slumbers and start to rediscover and explore your true nature and the higher purpose of your existence. When this happens, the matter and with it the soul's murmurings from within will get ever more powerful and urgent, for the simple reason that your energies are right for getting seriously started on the most important mission you have come to fulfill in your present lifetime. The time has come for beginning to save and redeem yourself, as this alone can set you free from the obligation of having to spend further lifetimes on the Earth's plane.

If that sounds scary, do not be afraid. Your inner teacher, the living God within, is ready to show you everything you will ever need to know. Don't be cross with your soul. For as long as you had no idea of what is in store for you and how your Highest Self is waiting to help you achieve it, what could it do but send ever stronger signals, until in the end you did come down with one of the above mentioned mysterious illnesses? Accept that this is the Universe's way of supplying you with sufficient time for looking inside and getting in touch with your higher nature.

However, if you wish to remain as closed off as you probably are at present and unwilling to respond to your spirit and soul's call, you will be in danger of wasting a whole lifetime that could bring you closer to humankind's dream of needing no further earthly lessons and moving on to higher levels of experience and learning. Think carefully! Do you really want to deny yourself such opportunities when they are on offer to you? Knowing what is coming your way here, do not give in to chemically suppressing your Highest Self's signals, when they are coming ever more strongly to you through the world of your feelings. Ask God and the Angels to help you find alternative healing methods.

I have been there and have done it, so I know how difficult this is and also that it can be done. I belong to the Prozac generation and remember only too well how the medical profession handed this potent psychotherapeutic drug out like Smarties. Prozac was claimed to be non-addictive by its manufacturers. Alas, it turned eventually out that exactly the opposite was true. Twice I have weaned myself from this drug. Taking it the second time was the very last thing on this Earth I wanted to do, but at that time things got so bad that in the end I decided to take it once more. I was hoping that it would only be for a while and that I would again succeed in weaning myself, which I did.

This is my prayer: I wish all the best to those who are struggling with this part of their journey of discovery and healing. May the Lord Christ Jesus, the highest Star and the brightest Light in the whole of Creation shine upon you, to bless and heal you and keep you safe, now and forever. Amen

M.W.J.

Entering the Doors of my Subconscious Mind

                        I am darker than the night,
                        Moving fast as the light.

                        I am stealthy, I am sleek,
                        Skipping above mountain peaks.

                        No human hand can make me.
                        No earthly band can raid me.

                        Built am I to navigate dimensions,
                        Programmed for instant ascension.

I float on the waves of magnetic fields,
Invisibly insulated within an impenetrable shield.

                        Welcome aboard - don't be frightened.
                        Try not to focus on the prismatic lighting.

                        Are you surprised I can speak?
                        Just one of my incredible feats.

            Do you recall your entry here?
            On your way up, you looked quite scared.

                        Feel free to scan and explore.
                        I invite you to walk my corridors.

                        Just one exception,
                        There are windows to your right.
                        Resist the temptation
                        To take a peek inside.

There are activities
That you would do well to miss.

As it's said on your planet,
"Ignorance is bliss."

You have an escort
To lead you by the arm.
He won't utter a word,
Nor do you any harm.

                Do not even try
                To look in his eyes.
                You will be unable to turn aside,
                For your neck will be paralyzed.

You must trust me,
This is for the best.
If you see the E.T.,
Fear will arrest your chest.

Keep on walking,
Look straight ahead.
Try to relax.
My, your face is red!

                You are on your way
                To a special room.
                You will have no conscious memory
                Of the procedure done to you.

It'll be okay,
This I assure you.
It's not the intention
To in any way hurt you.

Go with your guide.
I'll see you in a bit.
To mitigate your anxiety,
The room is therapeutically lit.

Well hello again.
There's more for you to see.

You'll need to take a seat,
For soon we shall leave the galaxy.

                        We will achieve atomic speed.
                        If you glance out the windows,
                        Only streaks of light will you see.

                        During our flight,
                        There will be times
                        When we will instantly stop
                        And turn on a dime.

                        But this sudden shift
                        Will cause you no trouble,
                        For the cockpit, you see,
                        Sits within a gyroscopic bubble.

Like a sheet one would fold,
We will be traversing wormholes.
These are cosmic shortcuts,
And YOU will be in control!

                        That's right - you will be my pilot.
                        Don't worry - you can do it.
                        I have been programmed
                        To talk and walk you through it.

                        You've been chosen to control me.
                        .If you can move your extremities,
                        Then you can make me go

                        Focus right in front of you.
                        See that small device?
                        It's known as a *controller dome*,
                        And it is the key to my flight.

                        No need to touch it;
                        Simply levitate your palm above it.

It will mimic your hand.
Each gesture signals a command.

Any direction you want me to take,
Just motion that way with your hand.

We will cover distances untold,
And you will be in control.

We will even transcend time.
But afterwards you will find
These memories will be locked behind
The doors of your subconscious mind.

Thought of the Day

(one)

Journaling is one of the most emotionally relieving, stress reducing and kindest self love practices we have at our grasp. There is something about gripping a pen real hard and furiously writing down all the things that ticked you off today, or gently reminiscing as in a dream of the wonderful memories you made that day. Maybe your day was dull and boring and you need to vent or brainstorm about some fun ideas. Whatever it is journaling can be incredibly beneficial for several reasons

Thought of the Day

(two)

I don't know about you but being kind to myself does not come easily. I have no problem being compassionate and complimenting someone else, but when it comes to myself, now that's a true challenge. Journaling is a great way to improve our self esteem and practice self compassion. Writing about things we did that were positive gives us documented proof that we in fact are not terrible people. Next time your girlfriend calls you a bad name show her the facts! You can also acknowledge the mistakes you made, take a look at why and hopeful conclude that hey, I'm human, I will do better next time. I'm not perfect, but I can do good too. There is something satisfying about seeing your accomplishments on papers, almost like getting a certificate or medal. Hang it up on the wall and show everybody!

Smile

The ability to smile is one of the finest and greatest gifts God has bestowed upon humankind. A smile is one of life's most profound paradoxes. In spite of being extremely valuable it costs nothing. Precious beyond compare, like all the best things in life, there is no charge for it. Although it has no intrinsic value, it cannot be bought, begged, stolen or borrowed. It is a gift of love that can only be given away, enriching the giver and as much as the receiver.

> A smile is a vital part of life's magic that sometimes acts like a light that someone suddenly switches on in a darkened room. It can make the plainest face beautiful and even though it takes but a moment, its memory may linger forever in someone's heart and soul. It can create happiness wherever it is placed, in the home and between friends, as well as in business. It is a signal of goodwill between all

people, nature's best antidote to trouble that gives rest to the weary and brings a ray of sunshine to those who are discouraged and sad. No-one needs a smile as much as those who feel as if they had nothing to smile about. So, next time you meet someone who seems to have forgotten how to smile, supply them with the gift of one of yours and see what happens.

The law of the Universe is love and God communicates with us through people. A smile that comes from the heart is part of the universal language of love that requires no interpreter because everybody understands it. Such a smile comes from the God aspect of our nature and communicates easily with the Divine aspect in others. It opens our hearts and souls to each other and conveys the message: 'I love you, you are my sibling, and you can trust me.'

Sometimes smiling takes courage, because it makes us vulnerable and we open ourselves to the risk of rejection. But in my mind it's always worthwhile trying and each time someone returns our smile, the souls of both participants in this exchange open and they are looking at each other with and through the eyes of God. In moments like that we recognize in others the great love of our Divine Father/Mother, who cares for us especially when we have to endure pain and confusion, by sending someone along whose smile reassures us and shows us that we and our life rests safely in God's loving hands. Each time someone smiles a small piece of Heaven is brought onto the Earth plane that can be shared by all who know how to respond to it. That's how smiling allows us to take part in the goodness of the heavenly realms of life.

This is dedicated to my friend **Dwan**, who returned to the world of light this year. Yet, I have not forgotten her smile when she was still with us. It was sheer magic to watch her face light up. It made her look astonishingly young and it was easy to observe how her soul's secret beauty was radiating into our world, like a bright golden Star that lit up and warmed everything it touched. Seeing is believing and it was **Dwan** who provided me with living proof of the fact that human souls and spirits indeed are ageless and eternally young.

Who is Blind?

The one who can't perceive another world.
Who is dumb?
The one who fails to speak a kind and loving word at the right moment.
Who is poor?
The one who is plagued by too many desires.
Who is rich?
The one whose heart is contented

Dear Killer, My Lover

If you wake, you will not remember me. You will not remember you. You will not remember anything. So allow me to inform you on the subject of the summer that has passed, though my memory is still hazy. Where to begin? The day we met? The day we kissed? The day you stole me away and brought me here? The day I found a home.

After hours of meandering, wondering lanes, pathways, and tracks, which you drove along at such a speed, I wouldn't be able to catch a glimpse of our location (not that I could anyway, I was blindfolded). I just remember the soft gentle rocking motion as you drove the car up high into the mountains in circles until I couldn't remember how many twists and turns we had made. You talked to me along the way. Told me what was going to happen. I just listened. Lost in a deadly pool of my own thoughts. I was drowning. Now I am surfacing. When we finally parked, your rough hands were soft and gentle as they grabbed me and dragged me from the warmth of the velveteen boot of your Mercedes. You brought me inside the cabin, sat me upon a leather chair, and bolted the door hurriedly as if you assumed I was planning some sort of daring escape. How could I be? I'd never been to the cabin before. Silly boy...

You gave me a cup with a liquid inside as I asked you when I would be allowed to see again and you informed me that you would permit my sight as soon as I'd finished the drink. I began raising the china cup to my lips as you softly ran your strong hand through my raven hair and let it rest around the nape of my pale neck so its movement was confined. Gently you took the cup from me and raised its smooth china to touch my dry ruby lips and ignited an unblinking, unyielding spark within me, reaching every part of my brazen body. I drank the thick tasteless liquid deeply and your hand tightened around my neck so your fingertips reached my jaw bone. Lightly, you caressed it. Loved it. Needed it. Lowering the cup, you stayed true to your previous promise and undid the black satin blindfold with one hand and allowed it to flutter, with the sweet grace of a butterfly, to the wooden floor.I looked up at you.

Your eyes met mine and the fiery spark within me grew ever stronger. The blue of your eyes was the electrifying blue of a summers' day. I wanted to caress you. Love you. I needed you. And in an odd way, I still do. You gave me a strange knowing smile that seemed to glance right through my soul and I found myself smiling back. I did not want to smile back but something within my soul compelled me to. Of course, it was the spark.

You continued this for days or weeks or maybe even months, the concept of time is always forgotten in the end. All I remember was when you brought me upstairs, locked the door, and bent slightly and our waiting wanting lips made desperate loving contact for the first time since you'd taken me away. Since you had given me a home. Since that first kiss, we could not stop. We were addicted. At least I was. Not that I would ever tell you.

So allow me to fast forward, every day you had given me another cup of thick, frothing liquid which I drunk gladly, as a child, nourished by warm milk. And as I drunk, I began to grow weaker in my memories. I could hardly remember the drive, or the feel of the leather chair or even the soft kind love in your rough touch. But that day felt different. I was troubled. Something was about to change. Someone was coming for me. After our morning kiss, I heard it; sirens. The brutal deafening sound, so loud it reverberated around my brain until what little comprehension I had depleted. I told you we had to go and despite your refusing, I grabbed you and dragged you out of the cabin. I couldn't have you get caught simply for loving me. I grabbed your keys and started up the car engine. The sirens were getting louder more deafening. I drove as fast as I could up the trailed and tracks and pathways further until I could not remember where I had started.

Then it happened. My foot slipped

Me, you and the silver Mercedes flew until the side of the rough mountain. All I saw was your brazen body slumped against the dashboard. Still breathing. Then I was gone too. So I confess. Perhaps there were no sirens. Perhaps I'm out of my mind. Perhaps I tried to kill you. Perhaps I have succeeded. Perhaps I will wait here, staring into the mountains forever, dreaming of the possibility of jumping into the unloving depths of the beyond. I press charges against me. A life for a life. I cannot live in a world where you do not love me.

Until we meet in paradise,

Your Killer, My Lover ....XOXO

Idiot

Once, I considered myself
A smart person but now,
I consider myself
A massive idiot.
I am an idiot because
I am a waste of time
In everyone's lives.
Everyone may say
That I am useful,
But that is simply
Not true, in my case.
I am a useless, shell-shocked
Idiot.
Even though I'll get in trouble
For writing bad things about
Myself, I'll still do it
Because I'm just an idiot.
Of course, I'll do it.
Honestly, I'm scared
Of myself, of what I think,
Of what I can do.
I'm not just a peaceful,
Quiet person.
I am a burning flame
That won't go out

Because people just
Continue to add logs
To my crackling frame.

I am an idiot
For loving her,
Because I know now
That I can't have her.
I thought I got over her a
Long time ago, but 2 ½
Years of asking to date her
Just don't go away.
I am an idiot
Because I have that
Flame inside of me
Screaming at my soul to
Tear apart the asshole
Who stole her from me
After she's known her for

Two hours,
Every part of me aches

To break him in
Half like the twig

He is, but I'm not
A violent person, and
I'll never do it,
Because in this one
Single instance, I'm
Being smart about
My actions.
This is my message
To her, if I ever
Share it with her.
Thanks for ruining
That one shred of
Soul I saved for
You, of all people,
You back-stabbing,
Depression-inducing
Anorexic asshole.
Thanks for wasting
2 ½ years of my life.

Applause

If someone in your family tree was trouble,
A hundred were not:

The bad do not win—not finally,
No matter how loud they are.

We simply would not be here
If that were so.

You are made, fundamentally, from the good.
With this knowledge, you never march alone.

You are the breaking news of the century.
You are the good who has come forward

Through it all, even if so many days
Feel otherwise. But think:

When you as a child learned to speak,
It's not that you didn't know words—

It's that, from the centuries, you knew so many,
And it's hard to choose the words that will be your own.

From those centuries we human beings bring with us
The simple solutions and songs,

The river bridges and star charts and song harmonies
All in service to a simple idea:

That we can make a house called tomorrow.
What we bring, finally, into the new day, every day,

Is ourselves. And that's all we need
To start. That's everything we require to keep going.

Look back only for as long as you must,
Then go forward into the history you will make.

Be good, then better. Write books. Cure disease.
Make us proud. Make yourself proud.

And those who came before you? When you hear thunder,
Hear it as their applause.

Captured

Colour me craving, I am wide open;
Make me exhume a wildest desire
From every pore; this body of want
Yearns your all-devouring tempest;
The spark in your eyes of mischief
Divulge unrivaled bliss and torment;
Weapon of choice well-maintained,
So the trademark of a perfect killer
Slowly breathing in ecstasy's ether,
Lungs filling till a fervid combustion;
The all-engulfing flames of passion
With which I long to be acquainted,
Already haunted by the experience
Of ardent death in rebirth's premise;
Swallow me whole, for I am scarlet
Captured within the pristine of white

What is Love?

What is love?
You may ask
Is love us just living
in the past
Is love everywhere
Is there any love to spare
Should love be exclusive
Or should it be open
to every living thing that wants it
A boy asked to an elder and he replied
Love is in the air
Love is everywhere
There is always love to spare
Love should not be exclusive
God gave us love so we could share it

My Broken Heart

I lie on the floor,

Pretending your next to me,

Wishing there was something more,

I feel like I'm sinking in the sea.

I want to redo everything,

But it is done.

I think of the person you're marrying,

Knowing you're forever gone.

I start to cry and wonder why?

I thought your love was forever,

I guess it was only a lie.

Now I'm broken 'cause of your error.

Now I only want to forget you.

Music

The sweet, tangy guitar in country music. The delicate violin in classical music.

Music, music, more music.

I cannot live without it.

I always loved it, since it provokes so many mixed emotions in me. I love Pop, country, classical, light rock, Jazz… all of them. Except for rap. I don't really like how they're showing off by saying how many vehicles they have and they have least 2 million fans on Twitter (I mean, what's the point? Telling the whole world you are the best?)

I see hues when I listen to songs. Jazz is a midnight blue. Pop is a fiery pink-orange. The country is more of a "chill out" maroon color. As for rock, it's a light shade of green, with a tinge of blue. Electro is golden yellow, shining in the sunlight.

Music helps me focus, but not tunes with lyrics. I can't type and listen to two separate things. I can read in "harsh" (noisy) situations because that's me every day at home. I can't type or write in absolute stillness though. It makes me agitated, so music helps a lot in those circumstances.

When I have time, I'd draw of paint with music. Usually, I'd pick a type of music, then use the colors I see in my drawing.

Once, my friend asked me if I had to pick one thing in life to keep, and I said "Music and Art." I admired art since I was a little kid. I fancy

music because it's art. It makes me think of so many memories, so many feelings, so many souls and their lives.

People out there has suffered so much, gone through horrible things, endured the worst kinds of torture. But music.. it makes you float endlessly, with no up and down, no right or wrong. Makes you forget things, that make you lightheaded. With happy thoughts. Music helped me in dark times, cheering me up....... Music is the art of healing.

Pleasure

Our love of the erotic is what helped make us human. My own belief is that our ability to desire another imaginatively is not the byproduct of our imagination but the other way around. Our imagination is the byproduct of our sexual drive and desires—Eros. If a species doesn't procreate, then it perishes. Nature's trick was to use our imagination, to use our most potent organ. (As is often said: Sex is in the brain.) All our art, literature, and music is the byproduct of erotic desire. And that's hard for the many who conceive of the human mind as made in God's image rather than the fabricator of desire—or the devil's as some might say. So, while some quarters are still fussily censoring our erotic imagination, the world's earliest art, going back even to the Neanderthals, is erotic.

Opinion of the truth

Many of you don't know me, but for those 18 views who saw my view on suicide, this is for you and many more. I was called into my school's counselors office because of an alert. I didn't know why at first. I've been called into her office on only two occasions: needing an online class changed to direct, and for being "depressed."

I denied being depressed because I don't want or need help. I know that I will be flagged for this, but honestly, at this point, I don't care if they see it. I have dealt with being depressed for a while now, but that's the thing **I have dealt with it**. I never needed a therapist or pills to help me and I never will. I was told I needed a therapist because I have depression. Our counselor hasn't done anything but makes people feel worse from what I've seen and heard. I never feel super depressed until I go into that office. All they do is label you and treat you as a baby. I know they can help some people, but some people just wanna be left alone.

Many people have really bad depression, but help doesn't always work. I've never had help, but I know people and have heard stories of people who tried, and **sometimes** it works out. To most people the pills make you loopy, people treat you like a kid makes you feel worse, and therapy makes you wanna die even more. The rate of suicides yearly has gone up since we started to label it as a disease/illness.

Depression isn't a disease/illness and it's not going away because of pills and therapy. Society goes against you and hurts you. People leave and you get hurt, people bully you, your crush doesn't like you, death is blamed on you, anger is taken out on you, and there's so many more. I can't even think of them all.

The Haus of Vespertine

Darling deer, beasts of our love, we are gigantic. Wild,
we wield no pitchfork, no distaff, no broom. Women
are supernatural, especially one Lady called Vespertine but we
are more than that—witnesses
to great convulsions of nature. The hunters want to make
us less. Drag us through the fire by our heels to murder
what is feline in us, make fossils of our priestesses. Men
are small and call this power, but it's just weal or woe.
In the vales and shadows our bodies make, they wed
our girls turned doe, turned woman, some roam through the
shadows like the Lady Vespertine then doe, then woman familiar
with the Lady V and her dynamic doings are not these certain
shapes but the swift motion of their shifting. And we are craggy
hag's head cliffs, mist hanging grey at our chins, the saltwater
below and all it must bear, and what we cannot: men, marriage,
massacre.

"by Piccadilly Station..."
Act One – Scene 2
"the Dreams"

("by Piccadilly Station I sat down and wept" starts to play again as the nurse brings Rocco's lunch in and gives him his medication. Rocco takes the medication and the nurse leaves)

(Mario walks to the bed and sits next to Rocco. He caresses his shoulders and then gives him a hug towards his stomach area and kisses his forehead. Long pause as Rocco reacts to the conversation that happens between them.)

Rocco: (to the audience) Have any of you had recurring nightmares or recurring dreams? (Rocco has an improvisation with audience if needed asking about them) They say that these types of dreams occur because of unresolved emotional issues, that could have a personal meaning and can be highly symbolic. They are a way to protect the conscious from information that it might not be ready to accept. Like for instance, a Tidal Wave; it expresses the emotion of feeling helpless and overwhelmed and is common among victims of trauma. Or an empty house could symbolize feelings of sadness or loss or grieving for the loss of a family member. (in careful thought and then bursting in a cheerleader fashion) B-I-N-G-O…B-I-N-G-O…B-I-N-G-O…and Bingo was his name-O BINGO! AHHHHH…I think we're getting closer! Or at least I hope we are for that sake. My recurring dream or nightmare, whatever you want to call it, always started out in a far-away old dusty meadow. This pasture, in the middle of nowhere had a certain creepiness to it like I could feel the wet moisture in the air as if a storm was approaching. I had to find what I was looking for, find it quick and get the heck out of there. I always had this creepy feeling that someone was watching me. Was it God? I hope it was God. For God's sake let it be GOD!!! Or, was it the Devil, or Satan, the

Prince of Darkness, the Beast, Diablo or Beelzebub…the Anti-Christ? Ok, ok ok now I'm feeling a little freaked out, especially when I'm being watch by the Wicked Witch of the West over here. Or was it simply my quote/unquote dark side embarrassingly catching up to me? Sometimes I would walk for miles it seemed and sometimes barely a couple of feet before I stumbled upon it. Sometimes there was a path for me to follow and sometimes I was free to quickly move through the knee-high brush. I of course would often wonder what was leering in the grassy-grass; snakes, spiders or any other eerie menacing creature. (Rocco's body trembles and shakes of fear) In my nightmare, we'll call it now; depending on the situation I would sometimes see it peek out in the distance and then I would burst into this highly fast-paced jaunt, as if it were disappearing slowly and I was never going to meet its whereabouts. Or, at times it would just fall out of the sky and I would be standing right dab smack in the middle of it. Anyway, feeling quite better I am, in every dream I would come to its meeting, and finally…FINALLY enter this run-down old creepy amusement park. You know come to think of it there were many variations of this carnival I would encounter in these come-and-go dreams. They weren't always broken down because every so often a roller coaster could be seen running its course in the background or up-close as if it were going to smash right into my body. Hmmm…well, maybe that had to do with how much alcohol I consumed the night before. You never know, do ya? Anyway, back to my dreams, I remember that some of the rides would be rusty and far apart and sometimes they would be sparkly clean and new but tightly smooshed together like if they were all placed in a tiny little snow globe. I did have one dream where all these roller coasters and rides were twisted and curled around one another so much that you didn't know where one ride started and one ride ended…it was freaky. And, yes it was covered by a big huge glass dome.

(Mario returns from his lunch and kisses Rocco on the lips and stands next to the bed)

Rocco: So I bet you had a great lunch, huh? (pause for Mario's reaction) Mine was pretty good, you know the usual; salmon and rice and jello, coffee and soda and oh yeah soup and salad…can't forget the soup and salad. (uncomfortable pause as Mario looks through his tray of food) I'm just sitting here reminiscing over the recurring dreams I used to have about my father. (Mario's face turns to a questioning expression) You remember the nightmares I would have searching for my sickly dad in the amusement park and finally finding him at the station sitting on a bench slouched over as if all the wind was blown out of him.

Rocco: (back to audience) I had the utmost heart-wrenching visions of all. I was in search of the same person in all of my recurring dreams…(long pause and Rocco) MY FATHER…my father who had passed away. It all made sense to me now. I never really truly grieved the death of this incredible man. And in all of these dreams I found him barely alive sitting on a bench at what I thought was the Piccadilly Station. And I remember the dreams always ending with me asking him to "come home, Dad" (pause) "Dad come home with me, everything is gonna be alright".

Falling Slowly

There is no rope,

there is no light.

No more hope,

no more will to fight.

I am falling slowly,

there is no turning back.

My thoughts are unruly,

since my mind has gone black.

The darkness crawls over my skin,

like a disease out of hell.

I did not choose to dive in,

this endless well.

Losing all sense of time,

I move slow like water through oil.

The dark plays games with your mind;

An endless foil.

I give myself to you,

I accept my fate.

If Heaven is true, I will see you at the gate.

The Pure Dark of the Night

My family is shattered like a glass smashed by a hammer, these arguments brought up by my parents, the glass table shattered during those arguments, are still a vivid image of what I can only see when I close my eyes since that day.

The pain that pierced my heart when I see my mom crying in the living room as I peeked through the iron railing from upstairs was unbearable, just like grinding my heart on the coarse road of misery.

Years after years, the pure black of the night, along with the comforting stars always had me gazing at it, I always feel comforted when I see the stars get along so well, I hoped my past was just like the stars, getting along so well, shining so brightly, so beautifully that not only me, the others, could admire it too.

On a faithful night, while gazing at the night sky and into the warming stars, I closed my eyes, reimagining of how my past could be so happy and blessed, before I knew it, I woke up on the break of dawn, I could see the sun swallowing the night sky and the stars fading into nothingness, time passed and the stars were not visible anymore.

From that beautiful view, I got to know that happiness is actually everywhere, if it is up to you if you want to find it or not.

After that day, I did not gaze at the glassy night skies anymore, as I know that the comforting stars are everywhere, surrounding me, giving me courage, hope and happiness

Eternal Darkness

Eternally etched in my flesh of fire
Secrets lie hidden in armored desire
Ink screaming silently bleeds of addiction
Skin burning in sin cries tears of affliction

Expressions of rage masquerading as hope
Deceptions of innocence hang from the rope
Violations of youth sewn at the seams
Abstractions of darkness invading my dreams

Unleashing a plague of imminent sting
Releasing my demons on raven's wings
Halos of hatred haunt through the night
Chasing the shadows that taunt into light

Contradicting the violence I so love to feel
Wounds of infliction are not meant to heal
Badges of pain worn proud on an easel
Closure comes clean like a vein finds a needle

Courage

What if you have the only courage?
To get us through it all?
What if you need to fight harder?
Could you do that?
So the world won't fall?
Could you save a stranger?
One who could become your foe?
Could you sacrifice yourself?
And never let your rival win?
Could you believe you can?
Please save the world, my dear,
No matter how hard it might be.
You need to save me and all your love,
And the people you will never meet.
Could you do that?
I know you will become a hero,
But you need to believe,
That you have the courage

The End and a New Beginning

The Lady Vespertine stared at the sky. The world was about to end; the Big Bang was about to happen again. It was going to happen next to Earth, and it was going to destroy Earth. Everyone was visiting old friends, visiting relatives, saying goodbye. Everyone was scared, except for her. She wanted to see the Big Bang. The whole planet was going to die and there was nothing anyone could do about it- so why not enjoy it? It would be beautiful, Vespertine knew. A whole new planet - a whole new world. It may be the end of Earth- but it was a beginning for another world, another race. The Earth was dying anyway.

It happened so suddenly. One moment, everyone was saying goodbye. The next moment- BANG. It began. The Earth's atmosphere tore apart. Everyone was silent. Too scared to scream. It happened in slow motion- like stars exploding. It was beautiful. Then the next thing happened too fast- everything was blown apart. Buildings, people, everything. The Lady Vespertine's life flashed before her eyes. Then it was over.

The End

THE END

Table of Contents
Chapter One

Wildflowers..........3

Pomegranate..........4

The Little Ghost..........5

So Much Happiness..........6

Making Sense..........7

Silence..........8

Vespertine..........9

Gone too soon..........11

Continuum..........12

The Past..........13

Spiritual Infants..........14

At 4:00 pm. On March 12th. I wrote this..........15

Hide..........16

I am Nothing..........17

A,B,C's of Love..........19

Midnight and Shoelaces..........23

Your Peeling Skin..........26

Burn..........27

Toxic..........28

Trinity Guidance..........29

Hazel Eyes..........31

Love is..........32

Scars..........33

Post Diagnosis..........35

Me (to Be)..........36

Sp3ctum..........37

Children of the Sp3ctrum..........39

Black and White..........40

You were always more..........41

Breaking Hearts..........42

Rose..........42

The Silly Equivocal Thoughts I endure between Midnight and One in the Morning..........43

A Featherless Bird..........45

Chapter Two

Breaking the Mold..........51

Waste of Space..........52

LiveLoveLife..........53

What if..........55

The Wind (part one)..........56

The Circle of Grief..........57

The Wind (part two)...........58

Flowers, Moonlight and Breeze..........59

Kindness..........60

What can I say?..........61

Say nothing..........63

I saw and said nothing..........66

Lost in my Mind..........68

Two Moons..........69

Trapped in Today..........71

Heart..........73

Myself Burning..........74

Written in the Stars..........76

(A Child's) Reality..........79

Jungle Gym or Jim in the Jungle..........81

Space..........87

Sometimes when I wake up..........88

That Feeling..........91

In the End..........92

Fear of the Broken Hearted..........93

Inspiration..........94

The Deterioration of Bananas..........95

The Crown..........96

McDonald's is Mathematically Impossible..........97

She..........103

Spring Falls..........105

Pause..........105

Never Enough.........106

Pause Two..........106

Leaves Fall..........107
So Normal..........108
Butterfly Girl..........109
The Ballet...a Dance..........111
To a Dancer..........112
Spheres..........113
I Loved You..........115
Wen you Left..........116
I've Learned to..........117
My Prime Objective..........118
Exorcism..........119
Lucifer (and his own hell)..........120
To my Family..........123
Constellation..........124
Demons of Darkness...........126
Midnight and the Moths..........127
The Truths Surrounding the Utmost Exotic Childhood Snack...Fruit Cocktail..........133
The Gospel According to the Lady Vespertine...........137
If I were a Book..........139
Separate Self..........140
Sorry, Me..........141
Sorry, Me (part two)..........142
Your Heart, My Soul..........144
Sippin' Vodka..........145
Crickets..........149
Mask..........150
Love, Psycho and everything in between..........151
Undertaker..........153
The Funeral in my Heart..........154
Broken..........155
Design 101..........157
Depression..........159
The End..........163
We Die..........166
We Mourn..........167
I Think I'm Dying..........168
Bank Account..........172

Crown me with Flowers..........173
Touching Stars..........174
August..........176
Goodbye, Y'all..........177
(part three) The Wise Ones..........179
An Act of Kindness..........183
Taste..........187
Cold Dark Corner..........188
A Letter to Myself..........189
A Letter to Myself #2..........192
Down to Earth..........193
Eddie..........196
Black Box..........197
Parallel..........198
A Conversation with Depression..........199
Already Dead..........201
Wake Up, Mommy..........203
The Most Glorious Dream..........205
Devine Peace..........207
Must be Said, Must be Read (Part Four), The Wise Ones..........208
Entering the Doors of my Subconscious Mind..........212
Thought of the Day (one)..........215
Thought of the Day (two)..........216
Smile..........217
Who is Blind?..........222

Chapter Six

Dear Killer, My Lover..........225
Idiot..........228
Applause..........231
Capture..........232
What is Love..........233
My Broken Heart..........234
Music..........235
Pleasure..........237
Opinion of the Truth..........238
The Haus of Vespertine..........239
The Dreams.....241

Falling Slowly..........244
The Pure Dark of the Night..........247
Eternal Darkness..........248
Courage..........249
The End and a New Beginning..........250

CPSIA information can be obtained
at www.ICGtesting.com
Printed in the USA
LVHW090058160121
676619LV00002B/317